Suicide and Mental Health

SUICIDE AND MENTAL HEALTH

Rudy Nydegger

Health and Medical Issues Today

GREENWOOD

AN IMPRINT OF ABC-CLIO, LLC
Santa Barbara, California • Denver, Colorado • Oxford, England

Library of Congress Cataloging-in-Publication Data

Nydegger, Rudy V., 1943–
   Suicide and mental health / Rudy Nydegger Ph.D.
     pages cm.—(Health and medical issues today)
   Includes index.
   ISBN 978-1-61069-583-1 (hardback)—ISBN 978-1-61069-584-8 (ebook)
1. Suicidal behavior.   2. Suicide.   I. Title.
   RC569.N93   2014
   616.85'8445—dc23   2014021940

ISBN: 978-1-61069-583-1
EISBN: 978-1-61069-584-8

18 17 16 15   3 4 5

This book is also available on the World Wide Web as an eBook.
Visit www.abc-clio.com for details.

Greenwood
An Imprint of ABC-CLIO, LLC

ABC-CLIO, LLC
130 Cremona Drive, P.O. Box 1911
Santa Barbara, California 93116-1911

This book is printed on acid-free paper ∞

Manufactured in the United States of America

This book is dedicated to the victims, survivors, families, and friends who have been touched by suicide. I would never pretend to write anything that would take away the pain, but I hope I can provide some perspectives and knowledge that will help people to understand and deal with the issues that suicide encompasses.

CONTENTS

SERIES FOREWORD

Every day, the public is bombarded with information on developments in medicine and health care. Whether it is on the latest techniques in treatment or research, or on concerns over public health threats, this information directly affects the lives of people more than almost any other issue. Although there are many sources for understanding these topics—from websites and blogs to newspapers and magazines—students and ordinary citizens often need one resource that makes sense of the complex health and medical issues affecting their daily lives.

The *Health and Medical Issues Today* series provides just such a one-stop resource for obtaining a solid overview of the most controversial areas of health care in the 21st century. Each volume addresses one topic and provides a balanced summary of what is known. These volumes provide an excellent first step for students and lay people interested in understanding how health care works in our society today.

Each volume is broken into several sections to provide readers and researchers with easy access to the information they need:

- Section I provides overview chapters on background information—including chapters on such areas as the historical, scientific, medical, social, and legal issues involved—that a citizen needs to intelligently understand the topic.
- Section II provides capsule examinations of the most heated contemporary issues and debates, and analyzes in a balanced manner the viewpoints held by various advocates in the debates.

- Section III provides a selection of reference material, such as anno-
  tated primary source documents, a timeline of important events, and a
  directory of organizations that serve as the best next step in learning
  about the topic at hand.

The *Health and Medical Issues Today* series strives to provide readers with all the information needed to begin making sense of some of the
most important debates going on in the world today. The series includes
volumes on such topics as stem-cell research, obesity, gene therapy, alternative medicine, organ transplantation, mental health, and more.

ACKNOWLEDGMENTS

A book takes a long time to write, which also means that time is taken away from other things that one might want or need to do. I have the most valued luxury of having a family that not only understands why I am not always available, but also does what they can to help make it easier for me to work and write. What they may not know is how much I notice and appreciate the little things (and sometimes very big things) that they do to help and support me. I think they all know how much I love them, but I also want them to know how much I appreciate and value what they do, but even more importantly, who they are. I particularly want to thank my wife Karen, who tirelessly proofreads and edits every word that I write. She not only improves the quality of the work, but she also keeps me focused on the purposes of the book and the intended audience. Thank you from the bottom of my heart.

I also want to acknowledge my editor, Maxine Taylor, who has been there every step of the way. When she would see something that needed attention, she let me know—and she was always right. However, although she never intruded on the writing process, I always knew that she was in the wings and ready to help when needed, and I counted on that and truly felt that I could always depend on her if needed. As difficult a topic as this book involved, having the support I needed made it possible for me to stay focused and deal with the issues this book addressed, which was not always an easy thing to do. Thank you to all of you.

INTRODUCTION

Suicide is one of the most devastating and tragic forms of death imaginable, and yet there are references to self-inflicted death throughout recorded history. Some cultures consider suicide an acceptable and an even honorable way to die, but in most places it is considered wrong, bad, illegal, sacrilegious, and/or immoral. Although it is common for people to think, wonder, or worry about suicide, it does not mean they are suicidal. However, when someone seriously thinks about and plans to kill themselves, or actually makes an attempt to end their life, this is much more serious.

Occasionally, the act of suicide seems to be understandable and perhaps even a reasonable choice. For example, if someone is suffering from a painful chronic or terminal disease with no hope of improving, suicide may seem a justifiable choice. Unfortunately, most suicides are not that "understandable" and frequently involve young people whose lives are still ahead of them. The tragedy in many of these situations is that, with appropriate treatment and care, many of these suicide victims could be saved.

This book addresses all of the forms and methods of suicidality, and will explain and provide examples. "Suicidality" refers to the thoughts, feelings, and behaviors associated with suicide (taking one's own life). However, it is important to remember that someone doing harm to themselves does not necessarily mean they want to end their life, but rather that they desperately want to change, decrease, or end the physical, emotional, and/or psychological pain they are experiencing. When a person intentionally hurts themselves, we must consider the reasons and circumstances surrounding the behavior and then determine a plan of action to help them.

The book's first section explores many of the definitions and concepts related to suicide, including examples of methods and types of people who attempt and commit suicide, as well as how suicide affects different types of people and different age groups. Readers may be surprised by the variety of issues that are related to suicide and self-harm, such as the historical, cultural, and religious factors, as well as some of the motives people give for wanting to end their life. It is obvious that each suicide is quite unique, which makes understanding and dealing with suicide even more complex and puzzling. It is never easy to fully understand the pain and despair that leads someone to decide to end their life. Sometimes the motives for suicide are *not* based on pain and suffering, but rather upon completely different factors, which we will examine later.

The book continues by examining the various factors that can increase the risk of suicidality. Frequently, it is assumed that suicide is caused by mental illness but sometimes that is not the case at all. Some suicides seem completely rational under extreme circumstances, but often other factors, such as drug and alcohol abuse, lead to impulsive and destructive behaviors, including suicide.

The final chapter of the first section focuses on the prevention and treatment of suicide from different perspectives and will examine the roles of society, health and mental health care professionals, families and friends, and others in their attempt to limit the number of those who consider, attempt, and commit suicide.

The second portion of the book examines some of the controversial issues surrounding suicide, including present thinking and research; for example, is suicidality "crazy" or not? Is suicide *always* the product of a troubled mind? Can mental health treatment really prevent suicide? One specific chapter looks at the rights of a patient, including the choice of when to die, a complex and important question considering the legal, medical, social, psychological, cultural, and religious issues. Next, the book examines the roles and *boundaries* of professionals, family/friends, society, and the law as they relate to suicide. Whose job is it to try to prevent and treat suicidality? What can families and friends actually do to help a person struggling with suicidality? What is society's role in dealing with and preventing suicide?

The final section provides additional resources, including articles, websites, references, short stories, and personal accounts about suicide, which offer a more thorough grasp of the importance and complexity of suicide. Each of the resources offers a discussion of the relevant issues, implications, and suggestions for further study. I have provided information regarding suicide that represents the most recent research and clinical wisdom available. However, this book was not written for professionals but rather for educated people and students who want to learn more about this topic. As with any educational endeavor, the reader may finish the book with more questions than answers, and that is when tomorrow's scholars enter the picture, pursuing new research that will benefit people and society in general.

Overview and Background Information

CHAPTER 1

Suicide: What It Is and What It Is Not

INTRODUCTION

The topic of suicide often brings to mind a particular person who has committed suicide or something that has appeared on television, radio, in a movie, or in a book. History and the media provide many examples of people who have taken their own life and often for reasons that seem to make sense under the circumstances. However, in reality, suicide is more frequently viewed as a tragic mistake that makes little sense to those who are left behind. Following a suicide, it is quite common to hear, "Why did he do it?" or "She had so much to live for," or "Why didn't he tell us he was so upset?" When a person chooses to end their life, survivors and professionals are usually troubled by many questions, and this is true even when the person has left a note behind or warned others that they might end their life.

It is common for someone to think or worry about suicide while experiencing extreme circumstances; for a short period, it may feel as though suicide would be the easiest solution. Of course, when someone does commit suicide, it eliminates the possibility that they may discover an alternative solution to their problem even one day later. The finality of death guarantees the end to one's life on earth, but even if one believes in an afterlife, there is no guarantee of what lies ahead of us after death.

Often, when a person is contemplating suicide they are not thinking about the permanence of death, but about wanting the pain to stop. If a person who is feeling suicidal is asked, "If you could push a button that ends your pain and suffering and your existence could cease immediately with no one left behind to be upset or hurt, would you do it?" Often, the reply would be an enthusiastic, "Yes." The reality, however, is that it cannot be that simple and that there *are* people left behind, particularly those for whom the suicidal person cares the most. Survivors are often left with a lifetime of grief and guilt as they continue to wonder what could have been done differently to keep the suicide victim alive. A person who is overwhelmed with problems and is thinking of suicide is not considering the possibility that with help they could solve or eliminate some of their issues in the next day or two or that they will create more problems for those they leave behind.

Famous people who have taken their own life, sometimes for seemingly understandable reasons and sometimes not, include Kurt Cobain (musician), Cleopatra (the last pharaoh of Egypt), Ernest Hemingway (author/adventurer), Margaux Hemingway (granddaughter of Ernest, model/actress), Adolf Hitler (Nazi dictator), Jim Jones ("minister" and leader of the People's Temple who led his followers to mass suicide), Marilyn Monroe (actress), Dylan Klebold and Eric Harris (Columbine High School gunmen in Colorado), Freddie Prinze Sr. (comedian), King Saul (king of ancient Israel), Junior Seau (NFL player, all-star, and member of the NFL Hall of Fame), and Virginia Woolf (author and literary critic). Tragically, no single type of person is immune to the possibility of suicide regardless of their gender, age, social status, success, or failure. The majority of people under significant stress or trauma, however, do not kill themselves; this is why professionals and researchers need to learn more about suicide—why do some people follow through with a suicidal impulse while others do not?

DEFINITIONS

Most people are aware of the term "suicide," but additional relevant terms and concepts related to this phenomenon will help understand its complexity. *Suicide* means the active and intentional taking of one's own life. The person "means" to kill themselves and actively takes steps to accomplish that end. People considering suicide can possess many different and sometimes unclear reasons for attempting suicide, and while friends and family frequently question the motives that led to the act, there is rarely a simple answer. Some may wonder if a suicide was an intentional desire to die, an "accidental" successful attempt, or "a cry for help." "Committed" suicide is when an action taken results in a person's own death. Obviously, there are many more people who attempt suicide than who commit it, but it is important to remember that a prior suicide attempt is a serious risk factor for future suicide attempts.

Self-harm is intentionally hurting oneself in order to inflict pain and/ or damage, but in this case, not to the point of death. Although self-harm can lead to suicide, it is usually initiated by factors other than the desire to end one's life. This does not minimize the seriousness of self-harm, but it is important to keep in mind that any action of self-harm may be an indication of serious issues other than suicidality. It is sometimes difficult to determine when an apparent self-inflicted death was intentional (suicide) or unintentional (accidental death). When someone does not intend to kill themselves but inflicts harm upon their own body, there is always the risk of underestimating the danger of their actions and actually killing themselves unintentionally. For example, persons who engage in self-harm by cutting themselves can accidentally cut too deeply and die from blood loss.

Assisted suicide is when one person helps or facilitates another person's death. For example, a person who is suffering from a painful, incurable, and probably fatal condition is aided by someone to take action/inaction that will bring about the person's death. An unauthorized person "pulling the plug" from life-sustaining medical support technology, giving the person a fatal dose of some medication, not feeding them, or failing to give them water are examples of "assisted suicide," *only* if it is consistent with the patient's wishes. The fine line between assisted suicide and murder is determined by the courts, juries, and judges who have wrestled with this issue over the years. The major difference between murder and assisted suicide is the expressed wishes of the patient/victim and the laws of the state in which one lives.

The term *euthanasia* (sometimes called "mercy killing") refers to one person helping another commit suicide or aiding in their death. "Voluntary euthanasia" is like assisted suicide if it is performed with the knowledge and support of the patient/victim. Although this is still considered to be murder in many countries, including the United States, it is considered legal in some countries. There are two other forms of euthanasia that are illegal in every country, with some qualifications under certain circumstances. "*Non*-voluntary euthanasia" involves a situation in which a patient who is incapable of giving permission to end their life voluntarily but has no true quality of life—for example, being "brain dead" and is sustained on life support. The person may have no brain activity, no consciousness, and no way of communicating that they want to live or not, and someone else takes the responsibility of action/inaction that will end the person's life. Although nonvoluntary euthanasia is not legal in any country, it has been decriminalized in some, which means that facilitators may face legal consequences but would not necessarily be considered a criminal or go to prison. However, *involuntary* euthanasia is considered a criminal act in most parts of the world, and involves a person making the decision to end someone else's life without the victim's permission, and even if the patient/person is capable of making that decision. Historically, repressive political regimes killed those who were politically or medically inconvenient "in the best interests of the state"; for example, persons falling out of favor with those in power, or suffering from an expensive medical condition that might be drawn out for years at the cost of the state; these would be examples of "involuntary euthanasia."

Rational suicide is the act of a person taking their own life due to a decision that appears to be "rational" under the circumstances; for example, someone who is dying of an incurable, debilitating, and painful illness decides to end their life in a way of their choosing before their condition worsens and they become an increasing burden on family and friends. In this situation, they do not need assistance and could end their life on their own. It may appear to be a rational choice, but there are several relevant questions. First, is the person aware of all the relevant treatment options, including pain and symptom control? What if treatment was available and could make the person more comfortable and able to talk with and enjoy friends and family—would the decision be as rational then? What if finances are an issue for available treatment, but all options have not been explored? Or, what if the decision to end their life was based upon their depression ("normal" under the circumstances), and if adequately treated, they may not feel the same about dying? Prior to someone making the decision to end their life, it is important that each of these relevant questions be asked and answered.

A *suicide attack* is when a person attacks another person or group knowing full well that the outcome of such an attack will be their own death. However, this does not mean that soldiers entering into battle on a suicidal mission want to kill themselves—in this situation, the soldiers are placing their duty above their own lives. A specific variant of a suicide attack is referred to as *suicide by cop*. Occasionally, someone who is facing law-enforcement personnel will intentionally charge or fire at a police officer following the warning to drop their weapon. The officer(s) must then take action and possibly kill the attacker in order to protect themselves and/or the public. If a person wants to die but is not able to do it themselves directly, they may plan *a suicide attack* or suicide by cop to end their own life.

Suicide by "accident" refers to a situation when a person stages an "accident" that is not truly an accident, but is intended to result in the person's death. For example, someone commits suicide if they intentionally crash their car, or "accidentally" take too much of a particular medicine, or mix their medicine with alcohol with the intention of dying. The main difficulty with this type of suicide is that, in the absence of a note or other form of communication to let others know of their true intent, it may be difficult to determine if the "accident" was truly an accident or a suicide. Later, *psychological autopsy* will be discussed, a process that is performed when a person commits or attempts suicide to try to determine why and what happened.

Why would someone who wants to kill themselves resort to staging an "accident?" Perhaps the person wants to save their family and friends from the heartbreak and stigma of suicide, or a person thinks that their life insurance policy will not pay a death benefit if it is death by suicide, which may be true. Finally, the person may simply not want to be remembered as a suicide and may be trying to protect their reputation and legacy. Whatever the reasons, suicide by accident is still suicide, and an accident is still an accident—in other words, if a person intentionally kills themselves by staging an accident it is suicide; however, if they die as a result of a legitimate accident that was not intended to result in their death, then it is a tragic accident.

Murder-suicide is one of the tragic types of self-inflicted death; more tragic because it involves the intentional killing of another person or persons in addition to the suicide victim. Frequently these situations involve a failed relationship or a professional/educational failure; for example, a person is betrayed or rejected by a romantic partner plans to take revenge by killing the person who hurt them and then killing themselves. Occasionally, when infidelity is the cause of the relationship problem, the murder may involve the relationship partner (or former partner) and that person's current romantic interest. A typical situation might involve a jealous or rejected spouse who catches their partner in a compromising situation and kills the spouse and their new "flame," and then kills themselves. Murder-suicide has also been reported in work and school environments where a disgruntled employee (or former employee) or a student (or former student) enters a location and kills the person(s) with whom they are angry, or random people who happened to be in the wrong place at the wrong time, and then kill themselves.

Mass suicide is a situation where a group of people decide to kill themselves at the same time and usually in the same place. This is most frequently seen in the United States in a specific cult or group that is led by a very charismatic, manipulative leader who convinces people that they must all die by their own hand to insure that a specific goal is reached. For example, in 1978, a horrific event occurred in Jonestown, Guyana, South

America. The "Reverend" Jim Jones, who founded the People's Temple in the United States, attracted many followers by promising them a new life with a better future. When Jones claimed that his "church" was being singled out for being different and speaking the truth, he moved the church and hundreds of his followers from California to Guyana and established a commune called Jonestown. Due to the complaints and concerns of friends and family of cult members, members of the U.S. government investigated Jonestown to determine if the "cultists" were voluntary members of the commune or if their rights and freedoms as U.S. citizens were being compromised.

Congressman Leo Ryan from California traveled to Guyana with other governmental officials to evaluate the situation. At first sight, everything looked fine to Mr. Ryan, but before the congressman left to come home, someone passed a note to one of his cameramen with the names of people who wanted to leave Jonestown. The congressman stated aloud that anyone who wanted to leave could come home with him now; although many feared leaving and earning the wrath of Jones, a few people did try to leave with Mr. Ryan. However, Jones was not going to let them leave without a fight. When the congressman's group approached the airstrip to board their plane, five people including Ryan were shot and killed. Jones informed his followers that the U.S. government was going to come and arrest, torture, and/or kill all of them soon, and that the only acceptable plan of action was the "revolutionary" act of mass suicide. A mixture of a water and a powdered fruit drink (not Kool Aid as is often reported) was laced with arsenic (poison) and Valium (a tranquilizer) and given to all cult members, including mothers who gave it to their children to drink. Nine hundred and eighteen people died (including those killed at the airport), and of those, 276 were children. This needless act is a tragic example of mass suicide, but because of the manipulation by Jones and the killing of the children, many point out that it is an example of mass murder as well. Since many of these people did choose to end their lives intentionally by drinking the poison, it was a mass suicide for some of the victims at least.

Suicide by pact is an unusual situation where two or more people create a pact that is based on an agreement that, under specific circumstances, all of the people involved will commit suicide. Unlike mass suicide, where people die because they are pressured by their leader or peer, the suicide by pact is an understanding that binds people to the mutually agreed upon promise to commit suicide when certain conditions emerge. This "contract" usually involves all people in the pact, but it could implicate subgroups as well. For example, people who agree that when their government is overthrown by a rebel faction, they will commit suicide as a group rather than live under a revolutionary form of government. However, it is only a suicide by pact if the agreement precedes the conditions and if it is agreed upon by the members of the group. There are also cases where a couple that wants to be together but faces family opposition, creates a pact to kill themselves if they are not allowed to be together (e.g., Romeo and Juliet). While these types of scenarios make good stories and movies, they are uncommon.

Copycat suicide is described in the media and is frequently discussed in social networks. In this situation a person attempts or commits suicide because someone important to them has recently committed suicide. For example, when Marilyn Monroe apparently committed suicide in 1962, suicides in the United States increased by 200 that month. It should also be noted that her death was ruled a "probable suicide," and to this day there are many who still feel that she was murdered. Copycat suicide is also referred to as the *Werther effect* from the novel *The Sorrows of Young Werther* written by Goethe in 1774. In this novel, Young Werther commits suicide by shooting himself after having been rejected by his "true love." This novel was widely read and admired, and following its release there was an increase in suicides among young men who were "copying" Young Werther. When a person who is widely admired commits suicide, some "fans" or followers may feel that, if this person's life is not worth living, then their own is not worth continuing. Of course, the "role model" for the suicide need not be famous, but it is usually someone who is emotionally important to the "copycat." Many feel that copycat suicides are a bigger risk when media increases their coverage of famous suicides, and particularly if they portray the victim as a noble, misunderstood, and tragic figure. There are cases where the *copycat* victim seems to try to "get even" with those who seemingly caused the death of the famous person, or to hurt someone whom they feel was not suitably upset by the famous person's death. If the role model suicide victim is portrayed by the media in a positive light and their suicide is discussed as rational under difficult circumstances, then it is not surprising that someone in a vulnerable emotional state views this event as worth copying. Many cases of suicide by famous people include vivid descriptions of the cause of death or the method of suicide, which seems to invite copycats to repeat the act. This indicates the importance of events like suicide being reported factually and accurately but indicates the need to do so without the drama and emotional elements that often seem to accompany the news.

One type of suicide that is difficult to understand, and even more difficult to accurately determine, is the *passive suicide*. In this case the person is actually trying to kill themselves, but rather than taking any direct action, they will act in an indirect manner that will *eventually* lead to their death. For example, everyone should know that smoking cigarettes will shorten their life, but that does not mean that every smoker is trying to kill themselves. The fact that you will not die immediately upon starting to smoke makes it more difficult to stop, and most smokers will tell you that they plan to stop before anything bad happens to their health. Unfortunately, many people die every year because they do not stop smoking soon enough. However, someone who smokes heavily, with the knowledge and intention of actually dying from smoking, then it can be considered suicidal. Likewise, some people enjoy dangerous leisure pastimes where their survival is threatened. Of course, many of these people simply enjoy the challenge and the "rush" from putting themselves on the line and surviving. These "adrenalin junkies" will often tell us that they have never felt more alive than when they are involved in highly risky activities—they do not want to die from their activities but rather want to live to do it again. However, if a person undertakes these activities with the intention of killing themselves during the act, it is truly suicide. Unfortunately, it is often impossible to tell whether a death under these circumstances is actually a suicide or just thrill seeking for the pure excitement of it.

Bullycide is a term that has recently been coined to describe a suicide that is in response to bullying; this usually involves youngsters in the middle school and high school age group. Over one-third of teens report being bullied at school; 20 percent say they were severely teased; 18 percent heard gossip or rumors about themselves; 11 percent were physically abused; 6 percent were threatened; 7.5 percent were excluded from social groups and activities; 8.4 percent were coerced into doing something they did not want to do; and 9.4 percent say that their belongings were destroyed. Clearly, bullying is a serious and significant issue.

Victims of bullying are two to nine times more likely to commit suicide than youngsters who are not bullied (depending upon the study), and nearly half of the people who commit suicide are victims of bullying. Research in this area and concern expressed by parents, schools, police, and other authorities has necessitated increased investigations into bullying. A tragic situation occurred in Schenectady, New York, where several suicides of young girls occurred within a short period of time. Upon examination, it was discovered that all of them had been targeted and bullied by a gang of girls who had threatened and harassed the victims, both

Bullying is more common in schools today and is one of the risk factors for suicide. (Oli-veromg/Shutterstock.com)

physically and in social media, until they eventually killed themselves. In this present day of escalating social media activities, relatives and friends of children must be vigilant about their contacts and activities and keep an open dialogue with them in order to discuss and *listen* to the concerns and issues of their youngsters.

METHODS OF COMMITTING SUICIDE

There are as many methods for committing suicide as one's imagination can create, and some are more common than others. Depending upon the culture, gender, and age of the victim, as well as other factors, the methods of suicide may vary widely. Certainly, the availability of the means of killing oneself and the opportunity to do so also contribute to how the suicide is completed. For example, in countries and areas where firearms are easier to acquire, more suicides occur by gun. The number of suicides could be reduced by limiting access to this means of committing suicide. This does not mean that a person will suddenly stop being suicidal if the means are removed, but if limiting access *interferes* with the ease by which someone is able to kill themselves, it could provide an opportunity for someone to intervene and stop the suicide attempt. Typically, countries that report a lower suicide rate have a predominant culture that is very opposed to suicide, and/or the prevailing religion teaches that suicide is a mortal sin. Methods of committing suicide include:

- Bleeding (e.g., cutting one's wrists or other major blood vessels)
- Drowning (lakes, rivers, streams, oceans, swimming pools, and even in bathtubs)
- Suffocation
- *Hypothermia* (staying out in the cold to intentionally freeze to death)
- Electrocution (grabbing onto a "hot" wire)
- Jumping from height
- Firearms
- Hanging
- Vehicular impact (jumping in front of a moving car, train, etc.)
- Poison (most commonly pesticide, but also carbon monoxide or other toxic substances)
- Drug overdose
- Disease (intentionally catching a fatal disease—e.g., AIDS)
- *Immolation* (setting oneself on fire; jumping into lava)
- *Ritual suicide* (*seppuku* or *hara-kiri* in Japan where a blade is thrust into the abdomen; auto-sacrifice where a ritual sacrifice is performed to appease a god/goddess)
- Self-starvation
- Self-dehydration
- Explosion (e.g., a suicide bomber)

The most frequently used methods vary among countries, but the leading methods include hanging, pesticide poisoning, and firearms, depending upon their availability. In many countries, hanging is the most frequent manner of suicide and tends to be favored by men. Pesticides are more often used in rural and farming areas, where the chemicals are readily available. Drug overdose is also very common, particularly in countries with easy access to prescription, over-the-counter, and recreational drugs; this method tends to be more frequently used by women. In the United States, men tend to use firearms and hanging, and women tend to choose poisoning and drug overdose. However, when discussing an individual case, these statistics do not mean very much. Any person who wishes to kill themselves can select any method that they feel will accomplish the task. Considering the lengthy list of potential methods, it is clear that, if a person really wants to end their life, they can find a way.

MYTHS ABOUT SUICIDE

Recent research and clinical experience have provided us with a much better understanding about the myths of suicide. Some of the common misconceptions about suicide include:

- Myth 1: People who talk about suicide won't really do it.
  - Fact: Almost everyone who commits suicide has given some kind of advance warning or clues. Suicidal talk should not be discounted; never make assumptions about what you think the person actually means—if they are talking about suicide it needs to be taken seriously and communicated to an adult.
- Myth 2: Anyone who tries to kill themselves must be crazy.
  - Fact: Very few people who attempt suicide are psychotic or insane. Certainly, many are upset, depressed, and/or in severe emotional pain, but this does not necessarily indicate mental illness. Most people who are mentally or emotionally disturbed do not attempt suicide.
- Myth 3: If a person is determined to kill themselves, nothing will stop them.
  - Fact: If a person is committed to killing themselves, there may not be much that can be done to stop them. However, that does not mean that we should not try to intervene. The impulse to end one's life, however intense, typically waxes and wanes and may not last long. Consequently, an attempted intervention might be just enough to move the person contemplating suicide past the crisis stage and into a situation where they can receive professional help.
- Myth 4: People who commit suicide were unwilling to ask for help.
  - Fact: Scientific research shows that over half of the people who commit suicide had sought help in the six months prior to their suicide. Since it is very unlikely that the researchers were able to discover every incident of help-seeking actions on the suicide victims' part, it is estimated that far more than half of the victims probably did seek assistance prior to their suicide.
- Myth 5: Talking about suicide may give someone else the idea.
  - Fact: Although not discussing suicide is one of the justifications that some people use to avoid dealing with the issue, evidence suggests that one of the most helpful things a person can do is to bring up the topic and discuss it.

Summary

Suicide can take many forms and is often difficult to fully understand. Basically, suicide means that a person takes an action to end their life; the motives, reasons, and methods are many and varied, but the intention is to end one's own life. This complex issue has no simple answer or solution. Whenever you hear someone say, "All you really need to do to solve the problem of suicide is to," you can be sure that whatever is being suggested is not *the* solution. H. L. Mencken once said, "For every complex problem there is a simple solution—and it is always wrong"; this is certainly true of suicide.

CHAPTER 2

Who Commits Suicide?: Historical and Statistical Perspectives

The study of the distribution and determinants of health-related issues (including disease) is called *epidemiology*. This field deals with the application of research for the control of diseases and other community and global health issues. Therefore, an epidemiologist could study things related to suicidality and examine the risk factors to help determine which people might be likely to attempt suicide, and then be able to provide interventions that could possibly prevent suicidal attempts in the future.

HISTORICAL FACTORS IN SUICIDE

References to suicide are found throughout recorded history, and it is safe to assume that it was an issue prehistorically. It appears that, in the past, the main reason for committing suicide was to maintain or establish one's honor or to restore balance to society. Suicide also tended to escalate during times of war and natural disasters, and also increased during periods of shifting norms and values in society. Suicide might also increase during times of social unrest, when traditional societal expectations might not be as important.

The ancient Greeks and Romans had a fairly relaxed attitude about suicide, although even then it was a complex issue. For example, in ancient Athens a person who committed suicide without the approval of the state was denied the honors of a normal burial and was buried alone outside the city. In ancient Rome three types of people were forbidden to commit suicide: soldiers, slaves, and those convicted of a capital offense who were sentenced to die for their crime. It is likely this law was established for the

financial advantage of the state since the state would seize the property
of a person who was executed for a crime. But if they committed suicide,
the state could not take their possessions. Soldiers who committed suicide
were removing themselves from military duty, depriving the military of
their service, and requiring the military to pay to replace them. Likewise,
if a slave committed suicide, they were depriving their owner of their services. Rome did, however, approve of "patriotic suicide," which was to
commit suicide rather than face dishonor.

In ancient India, there were two forms of suicide practiced by women
as a means of "supporting" the memories of their men. *Jauhar* was a form
of mass suicide by women of a community when their menfolk suffered a
defeat in battle, and *Sati* was performed by a woman who threw herself on
the funeral pyre of her dead husband or following his cremation as a way
of honoring his memory.

Most of the ancient Greek philosophers were opposed to suicide including Socrates, Plato, and Pythagoras, although their reasons tended to be
more philosophical than moral. The Greco-Roman philosophers, "Stoics,"
saw suicide as an issue of free will. If a person committed suicide, they
were choosing to honorably free themselves from an intolerable existence,
but the philosophers called "Sophists" opposed suicide if it were attempted
for selfish or dishonorable reasons. Aristotle thought that suicide to avoid
debt, pain, or desire was unmanly or cowardly, although he did believe
that it was acceptable if the state ordered it. Interestingly, Socrates was
opposed to suicide and felt that someone who committed suicide would
be condemned by God. However, he did feel that if God "compelled" a
person to kill themselves, or if it was ordered by the state, then it was
acceptable. In reality, Socrates was ordered by the state to commit suicide
by drinking hemlock (a poison), which he did apparently willingly. He
had been convicted of "corrupting youth" and "impiety." It seems that he
was teaching young men ideas about religion that differed from the state's
approved doctrines; since he would not change his methods or admit his
guilt, he was ordered to drink the poison.

From the beginning of the Christian era, suicide was considered sinful.
As early as 452 CE (Current Era, formerly AD) at the Council of Arles,
suicide was portrayed as a mortal sin and the work of the devil. During
the Middle Ages, controversy persisted over whether or not one's search
for martyrdom was actually suicidal, but the Church remained strong in its
belief that killing oneself, with the singular goal of dying (without other
considerations, such as martyrdom) was sinful. However, continuing questions throughout Europe regarding the issue of suicide remained, although
there were some clarifications that emerged later in the 17th century.

In France, there was less ambiguity about suicide; in 1670, Louis XIV decreed that, if a person committed suicide, the body would be dragged through the streets face down, and then hung or thrown on a garbage heap. Further, all of the person's property would be seized by the State. Historically, the Christian church maintained that persons who attempted suicide were excommunicated, and those who died by suicide were buried outside of consecrated graveyards without markers or tribute. During the late 19th century in Great Britain, attempted suicide was deemed the equivalent to attempted murder and could be punished by hanging (perhaps they did not see the irony in this!). Interestingly, even in the United States people on death row may be placed on suicide watch to prevent them from killing themselves. However, in the 19th century, Europe's attitude toward suicide shifted from being viewed as a sin to being the result of insanity.

More modern, but still historical, perspectives include important and respected sources such as sociologist Emile Durkheim and psychoanalyst Sigmund Freud. Durkheim believed that there were four basic forms of suicide:

- *Altruistic suicide*—for example, *hara-kiri* performed to protect one's honor for self and family
- *Egoistic suicide*—a person loses social supports and cannot face things alone
- *Anomic suicide*—a person experiences a marked disruption in their life; for example, losing a job, home, family member
- *Fatalistic suicide*—a person loses control over their own destiny; for example, suicide is initiated by membership in a cult

Sigmund Freud believed that suicide was based on subconscious hostility that was directed toward the self. Not being aware of the basis of this hostility, a person develops a desire to aggress against themselves by committing suicide.

STATISTICS ON SUICIDE

Suicide around the World

Approximately 0.5 percent to 1.4 percent of the world's population ends their lives by committing suicide. Global statistics from 2009 list suicide as the tenth leading cause of death with about 800,000 to 1,000,000 dying annually; this means a *mortality rate* (the number of people dying from a given condition/situation) of about 11.6 per 100,000 persons per year. In addition, the world's suicide rate steadily increased by 60 percent between

1960 and 2012, especially in developing countries. However, it is true that the methods of reporting suicides have improved, along with technology, and that the "reported rate" has probably increased more than the "actual rate" of suicide. Also, some "accidents" are probably suicides, but this is usually difficult to determine. The increase in suicides is even more sobering when it is realized that, for every person who commits suicide, there are 10–40 unsuccessful attempts.

Suicide rates differ significantly between countries and over time. In 2008, the percentage of suicidal deaths relative to all types of death around the world were: Africa 0.5 percent; Southeast Asia 1.9 percent; the Americas 1.2 percent; and Europe 1.4 percent. In terms of suicides per 100,000 people in specific countries, the reported rates are Australia 8.6; Canada 11.1; China 12.7; India 23.3; United Kingdom 7.6; and the United States 11.4. Similar to the rest of the world, suicide in the United States is the 10th leading cause of death, with about 36,000 people dying of suicide annually, an average of one suicide every 15 minutes. Further, in the

Any group of people can have risks for suicide, but it is one of the leading causes of death among high school and college students. (Yanming Zhang/Dreamstime .com)

United States suicide is the eighth leading cause of death among males, the third leading cause of death among 15–24 year olds, and the second leading cause of death among U.S. college students. Also, in the United States about 650,000 attempted suicides are reported by emergency departments in health care facilities annually. Lithuania, Japan, and Hungary have the highest rates of suicide, but due to the size of their populations China and India report the largest number of people committing suicide, which accounts for over half of the suicides worldwide annually; in China suicide is the fifth leading cause of death.

Suicide and Gender

In the Western world men die from suicide four to five times more often than women, although women attempt it about four times more frequently and are more likely to report suicidal thoughts. This gender difference is even more pronounced among men over 65, where the suicide rate is 10 times more than that of women. One of the main reasons for this disparity is that men tend to use more lethal methods with 56 percent of males using firearms, and 37.4 percent of women using poison.

China has one of the highest suicide rates for women in the world, and it is the only country where the rate is higher for women than for men. In the eastern Mediterranean, the suicide rate between men and women is approximately the same. The country reporting the highest suicide for women is South Korea, with 22 per 100,000 female deaths; higher rates for female suicides are generally reported in other parts of Southeast Asia and the Western Pacific.

Suicide and Age

Adolescents and young adults are often considered a high-risk group for suicide, with it being the third leading cause of death among 15–24 year olds. It is also the fourth leading cause of death among people aged 35–54 years, and the eighth leading cause for those aged 55–64 years. The prevalence of suicidal thoughts, suicide planning, and suicide attempts is significantly higher among young adults in the 18–29 year age group than in adults over 30.

One troubling fact is the increase in suicide attempts within the younger age groups. Examples of suicide attempts in children aged two to five years have been reported, and even if they are not successful, some children are left with severe injuries. There has also been a 40 percent increase in suicide in the 15–24 age group within the past decade (males 50% increase, females 12% increase), but in many countries the rate of suicide is highest in the middle aged or elderly.

An additional finding recently discussed by the Center for Disease Control and Prevention (CDC) is that the suicide rate is also increasing in middle-aged Americans. Their data shows that in the 35–64 year age group suicide rates jumped from 13.7 suicides per 100,000 in the population to 17.6, a 29 percent increase. Nationally in the United States suicide deaths have exceeded deaths from motor vehicle accidents. Clearly, not only are suicides increasing but they are increasing in most age groups.

Suicide Crisis on Campus?

While, suicide is the third leading cause of death for 15–24 year olds, it is the second leading cause of death for college students with 1,000 college students per year committing suicide. Some data suggests that suicide rates are not that different between college students and persons in the same age group who are not in college. This may be due to fewer males attending college and to access to firearms beings more difficult on college campuses than in communities in general (notwithstanding some of the recent tragedies on campuses). Most campuses are taking aggressive action and are instituting a variety of support services and suicide-prevention programs. For example, Cornell University experienced a cluster of suicides in 1990, and again in 2009, when six students committed suicide. They have established a very active suicide-prevention program, as well as other relevant professional services.

Many of the studies that have been done consider undergraduate students (usually the first two to four years of college when students are working toward an associate's or a bachelor's degree) and graduate students who are working on a master's, doctorate, or professional degree. These studies demonstrate that over 50 percent of undergraduate and graduate students report suicidal thoughts and over 15 percent of graduate students and 18 percent of undergraduate students have contemplated suicide in the past year. Of those who thought about suicide:

- More than 92 percent of undergraduate and 90 percent of graduate students had a specific plan for killing themselves (drug and/or alcohol overdose were the most common plans).
- Fourteen percent of undergraduate and 8 percent of graduate students had made an attempt.
- Twenty-three percent of undergraduate and 27 percent of graduate students who had made an unsuccessful attempt planned to try again.

In the undergraduate student population the most common stated reasons for attempting to commit suicide include:

- Relief from emotional or physical pain
- Problem with romantic relationships
- Desire to end one's life
- School problems
- Friend problems
- Family problems
- Financial problems

One troubling fact related to suicide among college students is that almost half of them decided not to tell anyone. The main reasons why they decided not to disclose their suicidal intentions involved:

- Fear of being stigmatized or judged
- Being a burden
- Being expelled from school
- Being forced into the hospital
- Not having anyone to tell
- Sixty-six percent of the students who chose to speak to someone talked with a fellow student and *not one* chose to speak with a professor

One advantage of the college environment is that professionals and college staff are able to work with students in the environment in which they are living and studying—even if they live off campus. By having comprehensive programs that work directly with students and their needs, it is more likely that students will be helped and some future suicides may be prevented.

Racial and Ethnic Factors in Suicide

Differing suicide rates depend upon the country or region in which one lives and the person's racial and ethnic background. For example, in the United States, Native Americans have the highest suicide rate followed by (in descending order) white Americans, Mexican Americans, African Americans, Japanese Americans, and Chinese Americans. Among American Indians/Alaskan Natives aged 15–34 years, suicide is the second leading cause of death. The suicide rate among this group of people is 31 per 100,000; this is 2.5 times higher than the national average for that age group. Of students in grades 9–12, significantly more *Hispanic* female students (13.5%) reported attempting suicide in the last year than black non-Hispanic female students (8.8%) and white non-Hispanic female students (7.9%).

According to the CDC, the suicide rate among whites increased from 15.9 per 100,000 in 1999 to 22.3 per 100,000 in 2010—a 40 percent increase. For African Americans, the rate increased from 6.4 per 100,000 in 1999 to 6.8 per 100,000 (a 5.8% increase). The biggest rate increase in the United States was among Asian groups during the same time period with a growth from 11.2 per 100,000 to 18.5 per 100,000 (a 65% increase). During this same time Hispanics had an increased suicide rate from 7.1 per 100,000 to 7.4 per 100,000 (a 3.5% increase). Clearly the rate of suicide is increasing in all racial and ethnic groups studied in the United States, although some groups are showing a far greater change than others.

OTHER FACTORS RELATED TO SUICIDE

Some research has focused on suicidal rates in relation to a person's marital status. Across a lifespan the lowest rate is found in married people. Being widowed rather than divorced is associated with a higher risk for white men and women and for black men, although in the older ages divorce is a bigger risk for suicide than widowhood. Some may question why married people have a lower suicide rate, even if they are in an unhappy marriage; it seems that being in close proximity to others does have a protective effect. It is also understandable that people may react differently to the loss of a spouse depending upon how he or she died. Whether or not the surviving spouse becomes suicidal will hinge on their own personality and situation but also on the nature of the relationship and the availability of support from other people.

Specific high-stress occupations are higher risk for suicide; among them are law-enforcement personnel, lawyers, dentists, and physicians, with psychiatrists having the highest rate among physicians. These professions attract people who are intelligent and who also possess high expectations for success and competence. Psychiatrists experience the additional stress of dealing on a daily basis with people in very difficult situations who need considerable support and nurturing, and over time it often takes a toll.

Air pollution also seems to be related to increased suicidal risks; although it is unclear why it adversely affects the psychological well-being and mental functioning such as memory, thinking, and concentration, among others. It may be true that people who live in high-pollution areas are living in more hectic and stressful environments, which may also affect the suicide rate.

The issue of suicide is handled differently from country to country, as well as from state to state in the United States. Those states having the

Surprisingly, even the elderly, and particularly elderly men, may be at risk for suicide. (Lisa Eastman/ Shutterstock.com)

highest suicide rates (in descending order) are Alaska, Montana, Nevada, and New Mexico. Alaska has long, six-month winters where people are isolated indoors much of the time due to the cold weather, and it also has very high rates of alcohol abuse. In addition, each of these states has easy access to firearms. Some of these states have high Native American/Alaskan Native populations, which are at high risk for suicide as well. Further, these states are largely rural with little access to mental health services outside of the major cities. The lowest suicide rates are found in New Jersey, Massachusetts, New York, and the District of Columbia. It is true that their larger urban areas offer more access to mental health services, although they do have more exposure to pollution and the stress of living in a crowded urban environment as well.

Another motive for committing suicide in recent history has been killing oneself as a form of social protest. In the 1960s *Buddhist* monks in South Vietnam gained worldwide attention by protesting against the president of South Vietnam through self-immolation—setting themselves on fire and burning to death. Similar suicidal social protests occurred in the late 1960s when Warsaw Pact countries (those aligned with the Soviet

Union) invaded Czechoslovakia, and also in Italy as a protest against the Greek military overthrow of the Greek government.

During the Cultural Revolution in China (1966–1976) many public figures, especially writers, intellectuals, and artists, committed suicide to escape persecution by the *Red Guards* who rounded up people who spoke out against the government and treated them harshly. Some feel that several of these "suicides" were actually deaths due to mistreatment at the hands of the Red Guards.

THE RISK OF ANTIDEPRESSANT MEDICATIONS

In 2004, the Federal Drug Administration (FDA) put a *Black Box Warning* on certain *antidepressant medications* because it was feared that these drugs could cause an increase in suicidal thinking in adolescents and younger adults. There has been considerable concern and fear about this warning, but it is very controversial and is also misleading. First, there is absolutely no solid research evidence that these antidepressants increase suicidal risk. However, since several cases reported this phenomenon the FDA decided to put out this warning just to make sure that people were being kept safe. It is important to understand that the Black Box Warning does not mean that the drugs should not be used—rather, it simply means that if these drugs are used, the patient needs to be informed of risks and monitored closely (which should be done anyway). One consideration regarding the use of antidepressants is that they usually take a month or longer before the patient notices a therapeutic difference. If a person begins to feel suicidal after starting the medication, is it because the medication caused it or because it had just has not yet started to work? There is no easy way to be certain. Of course, if a person begins to think more frequently about suicide after having started one of these drugs, the best thing to do is to contact their physician who will likely discontinue the drug, and try another. Under no circumstances should all treatment be halted due to one prescription not producing the wanted results.

Patients need to be reminded that medication alone is not adequate treatment for depression and that it should always be used in conjunction with psychotherapy. By working with a therapist, the patient can be monitored even closer and the usefulness and safety of the medication can be continuously evaluated. Unfortunately, some parents and even physicians have become more reluctant to prescribe these medications to young people, creating an even bigger problem. In fact, since the Black Box Warning was first used, the suicide rate for the relevant age groups has actually increased. While it is unlikely that the Black Box Warning is the only cause for the increase, many professionals feel that it is one of the reasons. Remember, the biggest risk for a tragic outcome when dealing with depression is to leave it untreated.

SUICIDE IN THE MILITARY

In ancient times, suicide sometimes followed a defeat in battle, often to protect one's honor or to avoid capture, possible torture and mutilation, horrific deaths, or enslavement by the enemy. For example, Brutus and Cassius who were two of the people responsible for killing Julius Caesar killed themselves after being defeated in the Battle of Phillipi. Another example was the mass suicide by insurgent Jews at Massada rather than face slavery at the hands of the Romans.

During World War II Japanese units would often fight until the last man was dead, even in absolutely hopeless situations, rather than surrender and lose honor. Late in the war they also sent *kamikaze* pilots to attack Allied ships; kamikaze means "divine wind." As the war began shifting in favor of the Allies, and the Japanese were running short of planes, pilots, ammunition, and bombs, they turned their planes into "flying bombs" with minimally trained and often very young pilots who intentionally crashed their planes into Allied ships in order to try and sink them. These tactics reflected the influence of the *samurai warrior* culture in which death was seen as far superior to defeat and dishonor. In this culture, failure was sometimes handled by using *seppuku* (or *hara-kiri*) where the potentially dishonored warrior could regain respect by means of an honorable death, using a sharp ritual blade to stab himself in the abdomen. In fact, honor was so important to the Japanese soldier that it was reported that they treated the surrendered Allied troops poorly because they felt that their surrender was dishonorable and warranted harsh treatment. One story told of Japanese soldiers who sentenced an Australian unit to death in admiration of their bravery so that the Australians did not have to live with the disgrace and dishonor of their own surrender.

In recent years suicide attacks (often bombings) by radical *Islamic* militants have been motivated by the promise of eternity in heaven if they kill their "enemies." Suicide is not approved by Islam in general, but the radical Islamic *clerics* who organize these attacks do not think of them as suicide but rather as martyrdom with opportunities for the glory of God; they do not consider it a suicide due to despair but an act of selfless purity. Although this perspective is alien to many of us, and is frowned on by most Islamic people, it is the rationale that is given to encourage "suicide bombers" to kill themselves.

There are many historic accounts of spies from different countries killing themselves rather than being tortured or possibly giving up their secrets. Many even possessed the means to kill themselves if captured—often in the form of a capsule of poison that is swallowed. For example, Francis Gary Powers, a U2 spy plane pilot for the United States' Central Intelligence Agency (CIA), was shot down over the Soviet Union in 1960; he had a poison pin that he was to use if captured. However, he did not use it and was later returned to the United States in an exchange for a Soviet spy. Powers was later cleared of any wrongdoing by the United States and the CIA, and was given an award from the CIA for doing his duty under difficult circumstances.

SUMMARY

Given the multiple issues, motives, and variables that can affect suicide, it is important for researchers to find ways of reducing the risks, and for all of us to be vigilant to those who are at risk and vulnerable. How and why people commit suicide may differ from culture to culture and even from person to person, but the end result is always the permanence of death.

CHAPTER 3

Suicidality and Motivation: Ideation, Planning, Intention, and Commission

TERMS AND CONCEPTS

In order to understand how a person reaches the point of seriously considering ending their life, it is important to consider the various aspects of suicidality and the motives that underlie them. Suicidality includes all components related to suicide including thinking about, planning for, intending to, and committing suicide.

Suicidal ideation refers to a person's thinking about suicide even if they are not planning to attempt it. In 2008 and 2009, it was reported that among adults over the age of 18 an estimated 8.3 million adults (over 3.7% of the population) reported having suicidal thoughts in the past year. In another study in 2011 with students in grades 9–12 it was found that 15.8 percent of the students reported that they had seriously considered suicide in the past year. Although 8.3 million adults report suicidal thoughts, only 1 million actually attempt suicide. While most people who think about suicide do not actually attempt it, in almost every case of a suicidal attempt, the person had been thinking about killing themselves prior to the attempt.

Often parents are frightened and do not usually know what to do when they discover that their son/daughter has been thinking of suicide. Parents can reach out to doctors, clergy, counselors, teachers, friends, family, or anyone to help deal with an immediate crisis. Since suicide is such a tragic death and significantly impacts surviving family and friends, is it important to take meaningful and timely action.

Suicidal thoughts can arise from many different problems, but they usually reflect a person's overwhelming feelings that the issues they are facing cannot be fixed. "Hopelessness" is a feeling that is often linked to suicide since a solution to the person's perceived problems is not readily apparent. When in such a crisis, the person's thinking becomes so intensely focused on their difficulties that they cannot imagine a solution or the possibility that someone could actually help them.

Although thinking about suicide is a concern and may be a risk factor for some people, "planning" a suicide is riskier than just the harboring the thoughts. When a person gets to the point of actually planning how they want to kill themselves it is important to recognize the seriousness of the situation and to guide them to someone who can help. In the United States, about 2.2 million adults (1% of the population) have made suicidal plans in the past year. Also, students in grades 9–12 report that 12.8 percent had made suicidal plans in the past year.

The method a person chooses to commit suicide is often indicative of their motives for wanting to kill themselves and the seriousness of their desire to die. Some people who attempt suicide may be ambivalent about it and that it could mean that they still may have some feelings about wanting to live. Although they may choose a method that is less likely to succeed, the plans/attempts should be taken quite seriously. However, if a person jumps off of a building/bridge, uses a gun, or jumps in front of a train, it is clear that there was little ambiguity about to wanting to die since survival from these attempts is rare.

Some people who "play around" with the thought of suicide find it curious and challenging to consider different ways of killing themselves, but that does not necessarily mean that they are seriously considering committing suicide. However, that determination will usually need to be sorted out by a trained professional who can then recommend how to best respond to this apparent risk. This decision is not something a friend or family member should try to attempt, as this should be left to an expert.

Suicidal "intention" is an even more serious aspect of suicidality, and is beyond the point of just choosing a method to commit suicide. It involves the decision to actually attempt suicide. Intention is the step between suicidal ideation and action, and is when the person decides that they are really going to do it. When trying to prevent a suicidal attempt, intention is the stage where it is absolutely imperative to take action to keep the person safe. After the person reaches the intention stage, all that remains is for them to acquire/establish the means and then initiate the attempt.

Sometimes a person who is contemplating suicide will reach the point of intending to die, but then just before the actual attempt it, they will have second thoughts and abandon their plan. This is one reason why it is important to keep a person who is suicidal from the attempt as long as possible. The longer they wait, the greater the likelihood they will change their mind and not follow through with the suicide. Research has shown us that intention is a better predictor of behavior, including suicide, than almost any other factor. When a person finally makes the decision to kill themselves it is very likely to result in an attempt unless something happens to delay, interfere with, or help them rethink their decision and change their mind.

Attempting suicide is when a person takes some action that will or could terminate their life. Others can speculate as to why, for example, "He was just trying to get attention," or "It was only a cry for help," but it is never that easy to determine the true motivation(s) but it is important to remember that *any* attempt must be taken seriously. In the United States, about 1 million people report making a suicide attempt in the previous year (0.5% of the adult population). In all age groups there is one suicide for every 25 attempts, and in the 15- to 24-year-old age group there are 100–200 attempts for every completed suicide. In the 9–12th-grade student group, 7.8 percent of students report that they have attempted suicide one or more times in the previous 12 months, and 2.4 percent of students report that they made a suicide attempt that resulted in an injury, poisoning, or an overdose that required medical attention.

Committing suicide (commission) is the final stage in the long process, and the one from which there is no turning back. Commission means that the person has actually killed themselves by a direct action that they intended or at least caused to occur. A person can take decisive action and

Feelings of helplessness and hopelessness are often related to suicide. (Ken Tannenbaum/ Dreamstime.com)

intentionally kill themselves such as shooting themselves in a vital spot (e.g., head, chest, etc.) or by taking a bottle of pills. They might create an event that may appear to be accidental, such as crashing a car into a tree or swimming out too far at the ocean or in a lake. As long as these actions are taken with the intent of a person killing themselves, it is suicide. Others might decide to act in a manner that by itself might not normally be fatal, but because they place themselves in a situation where they would likely be killed (e.g., pulling a weapon and pointing it at armed police), then this could be considered suicide as well.

Committing suicide is never as simple an issue as it might be tempting to believe. Sometimes the reasons for suicide are obvious, but often they are not. It is usually easier to determine if a suicide has been committed by examining the particular method used to commit suicide (e.g., jumping off of a building). However, most of us have read a story or seen a movie or TV show where someone was murdered but it was made to look like a suicide—it is not always that easy to determine. Investigators try to determine if it was a suicide but looking for a motivation or "why." If there is a clear motive, it is often easier to put the pieces together and determine what may have happened and why; the primary question asked by the family and friends of the deceased, is often, "Why did he/she do it?"

MOTIVES

Some people commit suicide because of mental illness. A person who is severely depressed and feels as though their life is meaningless, filled with pain, and can see no way out of it, may consider suicide as a means to terminate the pain. However, if the reasons or motives that are causing them to want to die are due to a distortion of their normal thinking and emotions, then the actual motive for suicide is based on a mental condition that is probably treatable; with the appropriate treatment they may not ever think about suicide. In any mental illness where the person is suffering from serious psychological or physical symptoms that interfere with their life and happiness, considering suicide may seem understandable; however, if they received the kind of treatment and support needed for their psychological/emotional condition the person could improve and feel far less hopeless.

Physical illness or medical conditions (including injuries), particularly if they involve chronic and severe pain, may also be the motive for suicide. Still, important questions must be asked: "Can the condition be cured, stabilized, or significantly improved?" "Is the medical condition causing a mental condition, such as depression, which is the true basis for suicidal thinking, and might this mental condition be improved to the point where the person may no longer feel suicidal?" or "Is the person rational and competent to make the decision to kill themselves?" Even under what may appear to be obvious motives for suicide, it is still not an easy issue to unravel. Today, there are so many new and successful treatments available in medicine that in most cases patients can be helped to either improve their condition, control symptoms, or to decrease their pain.

There is one type of program that was developed to treat people who will not likely survive their illness. Most communities in the United States and many overseas have access to *hospice programs* of care that are intended to treat people with terminal conditions and who have a limited life expectancy, usually of six months or less. Hospice care is intended to help control symptoms and pain while allowing the person the best possible quality of life in the last stages of their illness. Some people have criticized hospice care for being involved in assisted suicide or euthanasia (killing a person who is hopelessly in pain and dying). Hospice is not about suicide—it is about a team approach to providing the patient with a comfortable life while dying from a medical condition. Hospice does not provide care to artificially extend life or to attempt curative treatment, nor does it seek to end life prematurely.

A new branch of medicine called *palliative medicine or palliative care* provides supportive care to reduce symptoms and to relieve pain similarly to hospice care. The main difference between the two is that the hospice patient is dying from their condition and the palliative care patient has a chronic or long-term condition for which no cure is available but the patient may not be actually dying of their condition. Fortunately, programs such as hospice and palliative care have significantly reduced the number of suicides that are motivated by medical conditions and chronic pain.

Drug and/or alcohol use are frequently causal factors in suicide and, therefore, must be also be considered a motivation for suicide. It is not uncommon for those who are addicted to alcohol and/or drugs to struggle with other psychological or emotional problems. Regardless of why a person begins to abuse substances, once they are dependent on a substance they have now created a new problem that will complicate their original issues, and particularly depression or other psychological problems. Substance abuse is considered not only a risk factor for suicide but also a motive.

Alcohol or drug use can create feelings of helplessness or hopelessness, which then might become the reason for wanting to die. One of the main reasons why this is a particularly dangerous problem is that alcohol and drugs often have a "disinhibiting effect," which means that behaviors which a person might otherwise avoid (e.g., suicide) are more likely to occur. The normal psychological processes that help people inhibit dangerous conduct are diminished when drinking or drugging, and an impulse to commit suicide might just be enough of a motive to do it. Unfortunately, alcohol and drugs frequently compound the challenge of avoiding suicide.

Trying to understand suicide is a complex undertaking. Each person is unique; each situation is different. While the motivations might seem similar, each case is special and like no other. Personal issues can occur in a particular cultural and social context that will also need to be considered. The person who attempts to kill him/herself obviously has personal reasons why they feel that ending their life is the "right" thing to do. On the surface their reasons may appear to be the cause for the attempt. However, their reasoning has to be studied in relation to their culture—is it a culture that considers suicide to be is wrong or sinful, or one that thinks it is acceptable and honorable? Is it a culture that gives people the individual right to decide to die? Does society foster feelings of support and help for those in need? Also, the family's culture and values are very important since all of these elements can impact a person's vulnerability to suicide.

Finally, social factors that surround a suicide must also be considered as contributing factors. For example, a person who is being bullied or abused may not feel that there is anything they can do to improve the situation and may see suicide as the "only way out" of unacceptably bad circumstances. Conversely, social factors can have a positive influence on a person who is vulnerable to suicide if their friends and family are aware of the situation and are able to come to the person's aid in a crisis. As a way of simplifying a suicide, observers sometimes mistakenly minimize an attempt as a "cry for help" as if that means it is not as serious as other motives. Persons who attempt suicide, even repetitively, do so because it is the only way they know how to call attention to their need for help. They may feel that they have not been taken seriously by those around them, they have not had access to professional services, or that they were unwilling to accept assistance even if it was offered. It is pointless to waste time trying to figure out a person's motive; it is far more advantageous to notify someone else in order to insure their safety. Even professionals do not try to sort out the motive during the early phase of treatment since the person will be so upset or emotionally blunted that they cannot think clearly enough to analyze and articulate their reasons. It usually takes a period of time before the person can meaningfully discuss their feelings and reasons for wanting to die. When a person is "crying out for help" by using a suicide attempt, the treating professional helps them understand how this method of gaining attention is dangerous and potentially destructive, and will outline a definite plan of action that will hopefully help. The patient needs to know exactly what steps to take should he/she feel the same in the future, and the professional needs to explain to the patient what steps will be taken on the patient's behalf. Only then would a professional begin to explore motives and to help the patient understand what led them to the point of considering suicide, as well as how to handle the stresses, pressures, and crises they may be facing.

In recent years bullying has been identified as one reason for the increase in suicides. Multiple examples of bullying can be cited in schools, in the workplace, in the military, and in homes where domestic or intimate partner violence is found. Often the victim of bullying is too embarrassed or too afraid of retaliation and does not report it to anyone. Documented cases of people being bullied and threatened to the point that they would rather kill themselves than continue to suffer the abuse or tell someone demonstrate the power of bullying, which also includes families where abuse occurs.

Although most bullying does not result in suicide, it does victimize many people and often with serious results and should be taken seriously. Sometimes victims who consider suicide fear retaliation and want to protect not only themselves but others who could become potential victims of future bullying. The message needs to be clear to everyone that you must report bullying in order to stop it. Bullies are usually cowards who use fear and intimidation to control others, and often work in gangs so that they can feel more powerful. Trying to handle bullies on your own only involves you in their game of power and control. Anyone who is being bullied needs to involve adults, police, and others in authority who can intervene.

Other motives for suicide that are similar to bullying are *prejudice* and *discrimination.* The word "prejudice" basically means "prejudging" someone due to the particular group they are associated with and is often used with a negative bias toward its members. Discrimination involves the actions people take as a result of their prejudice. Not hiring someone because of their gender or racial group is discrimination, while disliking someone only because of their gender or racial group is prejudice.

Victims of prejudice and/or discrimination will experience negative psychological effects, even if the victim tries to ignore it; this does not mean they will become suicidal. However, if the victim receives repetitive or serious comments/threats, it can lead to feelings of helplessness and hopelessness that may increase their risk of suicide. Intense and aggressive negative feelings in response to prejudice and discrimination can also lead to impulsive, violent actions such as hurting someone else rather than himself or herself. Others may reduce these feelings by taking a walk, exercising, visiting a friend, engaging in a hobby, shopping, seeing a movie, or any other healthy activity. Still others might deal with them in less healthy ways such as drinking, using drugs, overeating, gambling, overspending, getting in fights with other people who are not a part of the problem, or many other dysfunctional activities.

Interestingly, serious anger directed at someone else, who they are unable to approach or confront, can possibly lead a person to commit suicide as well. Feelings of helplessness and hopelessness about their inability change the circumstances or reduce the intensity of their own emotions may impel some persons to end the pain by permanently removing themselves from the situation. Humiliation at the hands of someone else is also a powerful emotion that could prompt the consideration of suicide. For example, employees and students who have found themselves in difficult subordinate positions have become the victims of suicide. It is important to teach our children and young adults who are attending schools/colleges and going out into the workplace how to approach superiors with respect and what to do if they are not satisfied with the result. Knowing how to handle one's own feelings of disappointment or vengeance in challenging situations can make the difference between forging ahead finding a suitable solution to their dilemmas and choosing healthier ways to respond to difficult situations.

However, in an attempt to "get back at" someone who has harmed them some might consider a *"revenge" suicide.* Not only will killing themselves halt their pain and humiliation, they hope to cause embarrassment or harm to the perpetrator who has hurt them as well. These kinds of suicides usually include a note explaining the "revenge"; for example, "I killed myself because person X hurt me so badly I could not live with the pain." But remember that this twisted logic has been created by persons who are not thinking clearly about the issues confronting them.

Earlier in the book, *"copycat" suicides* were mentioned, and this too can be a motive for someone taking their own life, and particularly if the victim is a famous person or a role model for others. People who are overly involved with the life of an actor, sports figure, or rock star, for example, can become so distraught over the suicide death that they may feel as though they need to die as well.

Likewise, when a person identifies strongly with a role model and has invested much of their own life in following and believing that they are actually "participating" in the role model's life, when the role model dies the person may feel that they no longer have a reason to live. Still others may kill themselves to "prove" how devoted they were to their role model.

Often, this type of person has a deep-seated hope that they will actually survive the suicide attempt and then be recognized as a tragic figure that was willing to die for the role model who has "defined" them.

Similar to the copycat suicide is the *"pact" suicide* when two or more people form or sign a pact that, under certain circumstances, the people in the pact agree to kill themselves sometimes at the same or agreed upon time and place. Why would two or more people agree to kill themselves if certain conditions were met? Is it due to an important issue or condition? Or is it due to the importance and power of the others involved in the pact? Do some feel it would be unfair or cowardly to refuse to join the pact and feel pressured to do so? Those that are hesitant to join in are the ones who will have real concerns about following through with committing suicide and fulfilling the pact when the time comes. For example, during the Jonestown mass suicide mentioned earlier, some people sneaked off into the forest and did not drink the poison; they may have been a part of the pact, but they did not follow through to the end like hundreds of others.

One of the motives for suicide that is always a concern is "manipulation." For example, the "cry for help" might be manipulative, but it could also be honest and legitimate. The crying out is often used by people who may not know how to seek the help they need. A person who attempts suicide purely for the purpose of manipulating others is not actually trying to die but is using the attempt to gain attention and demonstrations of support and love from others. Clearly, this is only a successful motive when the person survives. Often when manipulation is considered to be the only motive, it is usually treated as if it was not a serious attempt. However, there are problems with this assumption. First, what if you are wrong and they were not trying to manipulate others, in which case it is very likely that they will repeat their attempt with a stronger intention to be successful. Second, anyone who is attempting suicide "only" to manipulate others is choosing a very risky means. Numerous tragic suicides that were probably intended to be "unsuccessful" have been recorded. Mental health professionals will usually discover the intent when performing a "psychological autopsy," which often includes the contents of a note, a journal, a diary, or something else that conveys to us what the person was trying to accomplish.

Dealing with the underlying reasons for a suicide is challenging, but it is also a way to help us to understand how suicide can be prevented. Each person and situation is different and no two suicides are exactly alike, but the more that professionals research the underlying factors that drive a person to take their own life, the better the chances we have to intervene and prevent more tragic and unnecessary deaths.

CHAPTER 4

Risk Factors for Suicide

In the last chapter, motives for suicide were discussed, or *why* people try to kill themselves. While motives relate to the "causes" or reasons why, risk factors are affected by personal characteristics, behaviors, life styles, life circumstances, family issues, health and mental health issues, or any other things that can increase or decrease a person's risk of committing suicide. Persons who possess a variety of risk factors does not mean that a person will or even wants to die; but the more risk factors a person has, the possibility that they might consider suicide increases.

It might be easier to understand risk factors by using a type of medical disease as an example. For example, if one were to study risks associated with heart disease, they would find that one's personal history of heart problems, family history of heart disease, having high blood pressure, high cholesterol, high triglycerides, diabetes, being overweight, having a diet high in fats and carbohydrates, not exercising, having obstructive sleep apnea, as well as other conditions are all critical. Thus, having any one or even several of these risk factors does not necessarily mean that the person will develop heart disease, but the more risk factors a person reports, the greater the likelihood that they will contract heart disease. This same approach is true of suicide—the more risk factors a person has, then the more likely they are to attempt or commit suicide.

Many of the risk factors are similar to the "motives" or reasons why people attempt suicide, but risk factors are not the same as motives. Risk factors are the statistical factors that determine the probability that a person may attempt suicide. It is important to realize that it may not take many big issues to lead to suicide, but rather it can also be many smaller issues that accumulate to significantly increase suicidal risk. It is also important to remember that what might seem to be a small issue to some may be a significant issue to someone else. When examining and evaluating risk factors it is critical to determine not only the number of various risk fac-tors that might be present, but also the relative importance that these risk factors have to the victim—that is, not what others think is important, but rather what they themselves think is important.

MENTAL ILLNESS

Many people think that anyone who attempts suicide must be crazy. While this is obviously a gross overgeneralization and largely inaccurate, it is true that certain types of mental conditions do make it more likely that a person might commit suicide. The most obvious mental condition that is related to suicide is depression. While the huge percentage of people who are depressed will never attempt or commit suicide, it is true that depression is one of the main risk factors related to suicide. When a per-son is seriously depressed, they are often experiencing a very low mood and do not gain enjoyment from doing anything. Further, they typically have difficulties sleeping (too much or too little), eat too little or too much, abuse alcohol and/or drugs, tend to be socially withdrawn, are physically inactive, have trouble concentrating and paying attention, have difficulties with memory, and usually feel that nothing will ever help or improve their circumstances. Since these are also frequently characteristics of people who are suicidal, it is not surprising that occasionally depression can lead to suicide.

Depressed people will often feel negatively about themselves and guilty about real or imagined things that they have done making them feel like they deserve to die. Therefore, it is not helpful to tell a depressed person that they should not think or feel the way that they do, or that they are being irrational, or that what they are thinking or feeling is simply not true. Although it may seem as if you are pointing out the obvious, a depressed person has never been "cured" by someone else convincing them that their thinking is not logical.

Bipolar disorder (formerly called manic-depressive disease) is also a mental health issue that has a depression component and can increase sui-cidality. However, the manic component, or when the person is quite agi-tated and excited, could actually give a person in their heightened state of arousal enough energy to try to kill themselves. Bipolar patients have reported that when they begin to feel a manic stage developing, they decide to try to kill themselves rather than risk returning to the depths of depression. As with depression, bipolar patients are often at high risk for alcohol and drug abuse, common risk factors for suicide.

Schizophrenia is a severe psychotic disorder that is also linked to suicide. Psychosis refers to a disorder that involves significant changes in a person's behavior, feelings, and thought processes. Patients experience distorted reality testing, which means they have difficulty determining what reality is and what it is not. They often suffer from delusions (faulty and often strange beliefs) and hallucinations (false perceptions; e.g., hearing voices, seeing visions, etc.), and usually exhibit bizarre behavior and speech patterns. Schizophrenics often endure periods of time when they act more normally as well as other times when they are very disturbed. When more lucid and logical, schizophrenic people may occasionally choose to kill themselves rather than continue to live being schizophrenic. It is also true that some schizophrenics will commit suicide during an acute psychotic episode due to bizarre and distorted reasoning.

The accumulation of what may seem to be small risk factors can also lead to a significant suicidal risk. For example, if a person who suffers from anxiety disorder loses a spouse, begins to abuse alcohol and/or drugs while grieving in order to dull the pain, and then is presented with the tragic news that they have developed an illness, this might make them more likely to become suicidal. In fact, the anxiety disorder, in this case, would be the least risky of the elements, but it would complicate the picture enough to increase the risk of suicide. Thus, when many issues or problems accumulate the risk for suicide is heightened.

MEDICAL PROBLEMS

Many of us have heard or said things like, "If I were ever diagnosed with an awful disease, I would kill myself." While that sentiment might seem understandable, few people actually commit suicide due to a medical condition. My experiences in speaking with patients who suffer from serious medical conditions suggest that most patients are willing to do whatever they can to have the best chance of "beating an illness." There are so many new and exciting treatment options for many conditions that most people are not ready to give up until they have tried everything. I have also spoken with patients who, after undergoing lengthy and often uncomfortable treatment say, "I don't want to continue treatments and would rather enjoy the time I have left." Is this decision suicidal? Absolutely not; it is an independent choice made by an ill person who is choosing how they want to live the rest of their life, not how they want to die. Choosing to discontinue treatments that are no longer making a positive or curative effect is

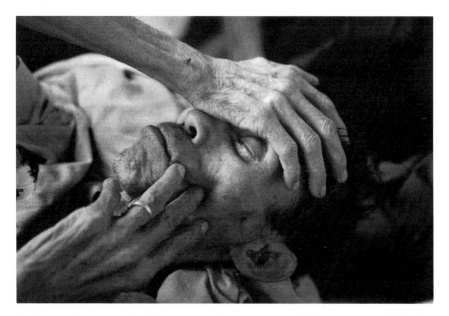

Having a serious or terminal illness may make a person more likely to attempt suicide. (Art Phaneuf/Shutterstock.com)

not a suicidal act. However, there are patients who have attempted or committed suicide, usually because they are frightened of the pain and suffering that might occur in the future and/or the prospect of dying, and this can be due to being ill-informed or not understanding the medical information that has been given to them.

Many people will prepare a "Living Will" detailing what steps of care are to be followed under certain conditions, such as a person being brain dead with no hope of regaining consciousness. It is advised that everyone sign a "Health Care Proxy," which is another legal document that indicates to whom the patient assigns the responsibility of making medical decisions for them should they be unable to make decisions for themselves. Many patients today will also sign a DNR (Do Not Resuscitate) order when they near the end of their life, which means that if a person's heart stops beating or if they stop breathing, other than making them comfortable, no "heroic" measures will be taken to keep them alive or to resuscitate them. Patients are being provided with better and more comfortable care than even a few years ago. Hospice and palliative care programs are good examples of medical approaches that focus on pain and symptom control rather than cures. These types of programs also concentrate on the social and emotional aspects of a patient's condition, and not just their physical symptoms. Research evidence states quite clearly that patient and family satisfaction with hospice and palliative care programs is very high. In fact, patients in hospice care tend to live longer than those in traditional medical care, most likely because hospitals are primarily focused upon treating patients and discharging them. Hospices are equipped to focus on long-term, supportive care involving family and friends often in the comfort of the patient's own home.

When dealing with a person who is seriously ill and suicidal, mental health professionals will respect a patient's feelings of fear, helplessness, and hopelessness, but while supporting the patient they will help them to recognize the realistic options that do exist and give them the opportunity to take control over their care and treatment. Many times well-meaning persons will try to make all of a patient's decisions in order to "take the pressure off," but by doing so they are also taking away a patient's sense of control and independence. I will encourage family and health care professionals to give the patient realistic options and choices to make—even in simple things such as what kind of juice they would like to drink. As patients feel more in control, even of the little things, it helps them get past the feelings of helplessness. Medical patients who are suicidal can usually be helped by attentively listening to them and their concerns and by generating realistic options and choices.

SUBSTANCE ABUSE AND DEPENDENCE

While substance abuse is a major risk factor for suicide, it almost always occurs in conjunction with other risk factors such as mental or physical illness, trauma, and/or personal and social problems. Alcohol is the most frequently abused substance that is related to increased suicidal risk because of the direct effects alcohol has on the brain; therefore, only a small amount of alcohol can result in a person finding themselves feeling suicidal. These same effects can occur with other illicit or recreational drugs and some kinds of prescription drugs. Each of the types of drugs mentioned fall into the category of "mind-altering drugs," which means that when you take them they affect how you feel, how you think, and how you act, and that is why people will often use and abuse these drugs.

However, these drugs can also make the individual feel differently in more negative ways. If a person is feeling depressed, the drugs/alcohol might make them feel better temporarily, but as the drug wears off the person typically feels worse than they did before they used the substance, and not just because of "hangover." The same thing is true of anxiety—even if the used substance makes a person feel more relaxed for a short time, as soon as it wears off, the person becomes even more anxious than they were before. The "disinhibiting" effect of alcohol and other drugs mentioned in the previous chapter is also one of the reasons that substance abuse increases suicidal risk.

In summary, the increased risk of suicide can result from a number of drug-related effects such as exaggerating the negative feelings that the person is experiencing, changing the way a person thinks about their life, their problems, or their future, or having a "disinhibiting" effect which makes it more likely that a person will impulsively act out, usually in negative ways such as attempting suicide. Clearly, when a person is thinking about suicide, alcohol and drugs should be avoid at all costs; unfortunately, when feeling poorly many people turn to substances as a means of finding temporary relief, which could then actually result in suicide.

PROBLEM GAMBLING

Problem gambling is a risk factor for suicide as well as being associated with other risk factors such as substance abuse. Some people with gambling problems may be successful financially and professionally, and gambling can threaten or complicate their financial security, relationships, jobs, and detract from healthier activities. Gamblers can overextend themselves financially with the hope and expectation that the next one will be the big win that will be the solution to all of their problems. However, what makes it "gambling" is that there is no guarantee that you will win, and the huge majority of people who do gamble extensively, lose money. The only guarantee with gambling is that if it is continued long enough, the gambler will definitely lose more money than was won and this includes playing the lottery. The miniscule number of people who win the huge lotteries might actually end up winning more than they have invested, but for the 99.9 percent of the rest of us, we are not likely to win.

The serious gambler is often someone who is deeply in debt and is receiving pressure or threats, is in danger of losing their job, marriage, family, and friends, and is beginning to experience health issues due to the unhealthy lifestyle that often accompanies the gambling life. Some gamblers feel that they have to act on that once in a life time "inside tip" in order to win a large sum of money that will pay off their debts and "fix" their other problems. They might borrow more money or cash in savings and retirement funds to put it all on one last bet, only to lose once again. Under such circumstances a person might become suicidal because they may feel as though there is nothing that they can do to improve the situation that they have created and that the only way to escape is to kill themselves. Recreational betting for fun with money you can afford to lose can be just entertainment, but for some people gambling can develop into a serious problem. Some people refer to gambling as an addiction, but it is not truly an addiction in the medical/psychological sense, but is rather an "impulse control disorder." This is a category of disorders where a person seems unable to control their impulsive behavior and acts on the impulses even when they know they should not. Researchers report that problem gambling has become a serious issue among high school and college students; a potential problem parents should be aware of.

FINANCIAL/PROFESSIONAL PROBLEMS

There are many examples of people who have committed suicide due to financial crises or professional setbacks. During the stock market crash of 1929, many wealthy people, and even more middle- and working-class people, lost everything—jobs, money, homes, most of what they felt represented the quality of their lives. Not surprisingly, some people felt that they could not possibly continue to live with the total loss of what they thought was important.

When a person's wealth and professional status are so important to them that these things come to symbolize what their life is worth, and if they lose some or all of that they may feel that their life is meaningless and there is no reason to continue living. Tragic examples of suicide in the professional world include researchers whose projects were cancelled prompting their demotion to a less prestigious position, or doctors and lawyers who lost their license due to a legal or personal problem. The loss of stature and prestige, along with a perceived lifetime of disgrace and humiliation has resulted in suicides. Once again two of the most powerful feelings, helplessness and hopelessness, can lead to a suicidal risk.

FAMILY/RELATIONSHIP PROBLEMS

Suicide attempts can also result from family and relationship difficulties, including the loss of a loved one through a breakup or death. Grief can sometimes seriously affect us, and especially if the relationship "defines" one's existence to the point that it results in that person feeling like there is nothing left to live for. Suicidal attempts following the death of a loved one or the breakup of an important relationship are all too common in literature, in the media, on the news, and in real life. When someone is seriously invested in a relationship and feels that it is critical to the "core" of their being—in other words, the relationship really defines who they are as a person—then the loss of the relationship can be devastating. When the ~elationship ends, the person feels as though a part of them has also died and that there is no reason to continue living. It is common for friends and family to say, "But you have so much to live for"; the serious issue, however, is that the person does not see a future for themselves without the person they have lost.

Other types of family and relationship problems can also be risk factors for suicide, such as relationships changing due someone moving away to school, taking a new job, getting married, or having children. They can so significantly change the nature of the relationship that the loss can trigger a vulnerable person to believe only the negative side of, "It will never be the same."

TRAUMA AND EXTREME EVENTS

While stress may be a contributing factor for suicide in some people, extreme stress that results from trauma or other crises is a common risk factor for suicide. For example, returning service men and women who have seen combat are higher risk for suicide than those who have not been in combat, and are certainly more at risk than the general population. The realities of the horrors of combat involve events that most of us will never experience; for those who have experienced trauma of battle, the results can leave lasting scars that may cause serious effects later. Although everyone experiences stress, both positive and negative, few attempt suicide. So it is not just the stress that leads someone to consider suicide, but rather how a particular person reacts to the stress and how many other risk factors are present.

Following natural disasters such as floods, earthquakes, tornados, among others, many people suffer from posttraumatic stress and other psychological/emotional problems. The mounting stress of multiple losses can increase risks of feeling suicidal or even acting on a suicidal impulse.

Typically, following the aftermath of disasters or major trauma, communities or governments may establish appropriate follow-up and support services to help people adjust to and cope with the difficulties facing them. Some victims need more support than others, including the need for a referral to a mental health provider. Although trauma victims may question the need for professional assistance, they usually won't argue that they have had sufficient past experience to cope effectively with a disastrous situation on their own. Encouraging persons to reach out for help because of situations that they have never faced before is not because the victims have suddenly gone "crazy," but rather because they will need to develop and learn new skills for coping with something that is completely new to them; that usually makes sense to most people. Resistance to mental health assistance is common because people who have suffered the trauma often do not want to think or talk about it, "I just want to forget it ever happened." Although it is normal for people to need some distance or time following a crisis or trauma before they are able to deal with it, it is vital that they do not substitute seeking professional assessment and care with only talking to family and friends. Fortunately, treatment for trauma is frequently brief and straightforward, but the sooner the person receives help (when they are ready), the shorter the treatment and the better the results tend to be.

In addition to natural disasters and other types of major traumatic events (such as the 9/11 attacks), a personal individual trauma can increase suicidal risk as well. For example, being the victim of an awful crime such as rape, sexual assault, assault, or others can leave a person feeling vulnerable and helpless. It is also true that causing the injury or death of someone else (e.g., being convicted of Driving While Intoxicated (DWI) or being responsible for serious injuries in another person) may make a person more vulnerable to suicide.

Other traumatic situations where people might consider or attempt suicide include being the victim of terrorism, being confined to a concentration camp or prison, or being lost or abandoned; any of which can result in having feelings of not wanting to live. Again, it is the cumulative effect of the risk factors that determines whether or not the person wants to kill themselves. People do not generally attempt suicide due to one solitary risk factor; it usually involves more than one issue.

Finally, a risk factor of great consequence that is considered a "traumatic and extreme event" is a "prior suicide attempt." Most suicides involve prior unsuccessful attempts. As mentioned earlier, attempted suicides far outnumber those that are successful. It is also important to remember to never disregard attempts because prior acts mean that a person is more likely to try again in the future; the more rehearsals, the greater the likelihood of completion.

Summary

This chapter has examined some of the risk factors that increase or decrease the probability that someone will attempt to commit suicide. Being aware of these factors and noticing when they appear gives us the opportunity to talk to someone who has caught our attention and express our concern. People should not "overdo" their concern nor "nag" the potential suicide victim into treatment—this not only rarely helps, it might actually make the situation worse. It is also can be helpful to discuss the topic with someone who knows more about handling suicides in order to acquire some ideas about things to do and those to avoid.

CHAPTER 5

Prevention and Treatment for Suicidality

"A suicide prevented is a life saved and a future preserved."

In dealing with any condition, illness, or injury, the best treatment is always prevention; if a problem can be avoided it is preferable to trying to fix it after it happens and especially since a successful suicide means that there is no condition left to treat. Prevention is very important to our general physical health, and it is just as important to our mental health. To better understand the role of prevention in suicide, it is important to clarify exactly what is meant by "prevention." There are three basic types of prevention: primary, secondary, and tertiary. *Primary prevention* in suicide is used when an entire population is targeted, and the goal is to reduce the overall rate of people who attempt to take their own life. Primary prevention involves programs such as Public Service Announcements on TV and radio, which can educate people about how to better understand the risks and how to obtain help for someone who is suicidal. The intention is to reach out to everyone who is watching TV and offer information that, hopefully, will reduce the rate of suicide within the entire population. *Secondary prevention* is used to focus prevention efforts on a group of people within the population are at high risk for a particular problem, such as suicide. For example, people who are suffering from depression are a high-risk group and programs are used to inform the public, as well as physicians, about the subtle signs of depression. Patients are often seen by their primary care physician (PCP) before they see a mental health professional; sometimes during a short routine visit, the physician might not recognize that the symptoms being presented by the patient are due to depression. Therefore, educating PCPs about depression and suicidality and providing them with the tools for depression screening, such as questionnaires, can be quite helpful. Research has demonstrated that most primary care doctors do not explore or follow up on depressive symptoms and rarely ask about or discuss suicide. More programs are needed that address depression and suicidality at the primary care level so that it is easier to identify suicidal patients at the earliest opportunity.

Tertiary prevention is used when a condition has already emerged and prevention efforts are designed to reduce the issues associated with the present condition and hopefully keep it from worsening. Obviously, there is no treatment for the people who have committed suicide, but there are certainly preventative efforts that focus on people who have attempted suicide and have survived as well as on people who are the victim's survivors and who may begin to feel like copying the suicide attempt. People who unsuccessfully attempt to kill themselves can participate in individual- and group-treatment programs where they are helped to understand how they reached the point of considering suicide. Professionals will explore each person's situation and relevant issues and will develop for the patient the means to deal with them more effectively so that dying was not the only option open to them. Although programs like these are available, often the suicide attempt victim, or their family, is embarrassed, frustrated, and discouraged to the point that they do not want to participate.

METHODS AND SITES OF PREVENTION

Society

In addressing the issue of suicide, it is important to focus on events that can affect society as a whole—therefore, primary and secondary types of prevention. By working with society in general, as well as the higher-risk groups, the total incidence of suicide should decrease. Suicide is one of those uncomfortable topics that people typically avoid talking about and, consequently, most people are woefully ignorant of many of the details and important elements of suicide. Some might question the right or obligation of a society to address suicide, but suicide is a public health issue that affects victims, family, friends, and the health/mental health care system. It is a public health issue because at every level of government from communities, to the states, and even the federal government the various offices of public health have the responsibility to reduce the frequency and impact of various health and mental health problems on our communities. In addition, when a suicide is attempted or completed, it does result in real costs that must be shouldered by the health care delivery system, such as the retrieval and removal of the body, the involvement of police, emergency personnel, and medical professionals, as well as the expense for family and friends who will need professional help in the future. Societal education can include television and radio Public Service Announcements, articles in newspapers, discussions in forums or blogs online, and articles and information sheets in magazines and journals. Schools can also educate and inform students, teachers, and parents about the signs of suicide. Some people might consider it risky or scary for children to hear this type of information while in a school setting. However, remember how the frequency of suicide is increasing in all groups *including primary and secondary school students.* A mild but informative program at school about suicide would be far less intrusive and upsetting to most students, who play and watch suggestive and violent games, movies, and programs on television and on the Internet, than to actually have to deal with this tragedy involving a friend or family member without any knowledge or preparation.

In addition, society can contribute to a decrease in the frequency of suicide by offering and paying for informative programs at libraries, community centers, school auditoriums, and religious institutions. Political representatives can assist by earmarking funds and taxes to help pay for these programs. Financial grants from agencies and corporations, as well as other fundraising activities, help to cover the cost of educational programs, which are relatively inexpensive when compared to the human and financial costs of a suicide. Early detection information for people at risk for suicide can be made available to the public through local mental health providers, physicians, and educators who are knowledgeable in this area and are willing to present programs to public groups for little or no compensation.

Since communities do not have an endless supply of money, priorities and decisions must determine where and how funds are spent. Should society spend more money on education or on improving roads and bridges? Should we pay for more military equipment and defense or for more social programs? "Prioritization" means listing the things that are most important first, followed by those that are not quite as important. Someone will always champion the issues that deserve funding, but a society as a whole must decide how it wants to spend the money, communicate the preferences and priorities to politicians, and then vote for those who follow through with enacting the priorities. Even those that are too young to vote can discuss their thoughts with their parents and other adults, and then at voting age they can make their vote count! If voters demand better mental health care funding, it would go a long way to providing ways to address suicide prevention more effectively.

Schools and other community agencies can have an impact on the prevention of suicide since they have daily contact with community members
and some who may be at risk for suicide. Schools and agencies are a good
place to start for early detection; teachers, counselors, administrators, and
others should know the warning signs of potential suicide risk, how to
address the issue with a person at risk, and who to call. Frequently, it is
people other than health or mental health care providers who are the first
ones to notice or be concerned about someone at risk for suicide.

Health and Mental Health Care Professionals

Health and mental health care professionals are helpful in identifying
people at risk for suicide and need to stay current on the issues by taking
continuing education courses, reading relevant journals and books, and by
being vigilant for signs of suicidality. Many medical schools and residency
programs are now educating doctors more extensively about the issues of
suicide, how to recognize symptoms, and what to do when they encounter
a person who they think might be at risk. "Should the patient be referred
for another type of treatment (e.g., inpatient)?" "Does the patient have an

Most people who feel suicidal can be helped by someone who has the experience and training. (Rob Marmion/Dreamstime.com)

immediate plan of action to keep them safe?" "With whom does care need to be coordinated?" "Who else (e.g., family or caregivers) needs to be informed and kept abreast of the risks and issues?"

Usually the PCP sees a patient who is a potential suicidal risk before any other professional. Frequently, the PCP is under pressure to see more patients within a short period of time and often does not have the time to assess every problem that people may have. It is still vitally important that the treating professional in the primary care setting takes the time to ask pertinent questions and discuss a patient's concerns with them, while assessing for suicide risk. The best advice for preventing suicide at the earliest opportunity is to listen; pay attention to what is being said, and especially notice what is *not* being shared. Often, the best source of information is the patient. As with many medical and psychological problems, early detection usually means better treatment results.

Family and Friends

Family and friends usually have the most frequent and closest contact with those who may be at risk for suicide. While most people who have some of the risk factors for suicide will never attempt to kill themselves, it is wise to observe them and to be aware of signs. The most important thing for family and friends to do is to pay attention to *changes in behavior*. When someone begins to act differently, it does not necessarily mean that they are suicidal, but it is usually for a reason. Some changes might include sleeping longer or shorter periods of time, eating habits, remaining at home more and missing social activities, going out more and avoiding being around family and friends, cleaning their room and throwing out sentimental items and photos, wearing long sleeved or bulky clothing when it is warm, missing school/college classes, not engaging in conversations, and anything else that could be considered *extreme* compared to the person's normal behavior. Obviously, if someone cleans their room and purges it of clutter weekly/monthly, it is not an extreme change. If someone who is shy has been working on getting out more socially, this is not an abrupt, unexpected change but rather a welcomed one.

When one notices a significant change in a person's behavior, it is appropriate to ask them if there is anything bothering them and to remain in close proximity for a period of time—especially if the answer is "no." Sometimes the continued presence of someone who seems to care is enough for a person to open up. Sometimes beginning a conversation about an unrelated topic allows them to become comfortable with talking and can lead to a discussion about what is troubling them. They may not be sleeping well or feeling well, or they had an argument with a parent, spouse, or friend. What they usually want and need is someone to listen to them rather than someone who lectures and corrects them or makes light of their concerns. Thus, when you are listening to someone, you should primarily be—listening. Ask questions, make positive comments, but the main thing to do is to listen carefully and attentively, which means maintaining eye contact even if they do not look back at you. Eye contact is a powerful, intimate means of showing concern. Physical contact, such as hugging, can also demonstrate support but only if it is appropriate in the relationship, and sometimes it is not the right thing to do.

Under some circumstances it is appropriate to mention your own concerns and to make suggestions. Another necessary course of action is to immediately contact an adult if you feel that the person is at risk and needs assistance, and if you are an adult yourself it would be helpful to share your concerns with another adult. Calling a relative, friend, teacher, coworker, medical professional, or a suicide hotline in your community can help you to decide the next step in protecting a vulnerable person. Contacting someone else for assistance may not be appropriate in their presence if it seems to you that the issue of trust and betrayal will anger them enough to leave. However, immediately calling someone is far more important to preventing a suicide than worrying about them being upset with you.

Proposing options to someone who is feeling hopeless is not always helpful because they have already decided that there is nothing that can be done. Most likely that is not an accurate assessment of the situation but making suggestions, listening, and not nagging them is a good place to start. Being there for support and contacting someone as soon as possible are the most beneficial steps one can take when dealing with a person who is considering suicide.

In today's digital world there is more information available than one can ever fully utilize. Reading and learning more about the topics of suicide and mental health are good ways to familiarize yourself with signs and suggestions about what to do to help someone. However, anyone can put anything up on the Internet, and you need to pay attention to the site address from which the information is being posted. Some sites are not legitimate, and although online sources may appear to be impressive, they can be completely bogus. At the end of this book there are examples of trustworthy and helpful sources for information about suicide for your use.

When listening to someone who is in crisis, it is tempting to give advice or try to fix the problem rather than turn to professionals, and especially when the person stresses that they will only talk to someone they know, like you, and not a "stranger." During a crisis, talking to someone with whom they have a personal relationship is not a sufficient substitute for professional help—*do not try to be the person's doctor yourself.* They need relatives and friends to be supportive and understanding, not to be their *counselor.* When a person is in crisis, and particularly if they are resistant to help, they may need to be taken to the nearest emergency room and a call to 911 is the responsible thing to do. It is better to err on the side of caution; you can straighten out the disagreement later. You would never treat a broken arm by yourself, nor should you treat a suicidal person alone. Even professionals who practice in the mental health field are advised not to treat family and friends in crisis. It is better to protect the personal relationship that exists by referring the person to another provider and not to complicate it by treating them professionally yourself.

Most importantly, be aware that you cannot take responsibility for keeping someone alive. It is unrealistic and impossible for an untrained, although caring person, to provide the type of treatment and protection that will meet all of the patient's needs. All one can do is take appropriate steps to let someone else know of the situation. Depending upon one's age, size, gender, and strength, that is all that can be expected.

Risk Assessment

Formal assessment of suicidal risk is only performed by a trained professional who has the knowledge and experience to do it appropriately. However, knowing how a risk assessment works can be helpful in understanding how immediate the risk might be. The first step in assessing risk is to determine at which stage of suicidality the person is functioning. Have they been thinking about suicide or death (suicidal ideation)? Have they formulated a plan for committing suicide (planning)? Does it seem like they expect to try to kill themselves (intention)? Have they actually tried to commit suicide but failed (attempt)? The final stage of suicidality is the commission of suicide, and if the person has already been successful, then risk assessment is already too late. Depending upon which stage the person is at will determine what needs to happen next in order to keep the person safe and to help them deal with the problem(s) they are facing.

The next stage in assessing risk for suicidality is to consider the opportunities that are available to the person. Do they have access to the means to commit suicide (weapons, pills, ropes, poisons, etc.)? Limiting access to these things is certainly one way to reduce risk. Other aspects of the situation must be considered such as "How often are they left alone?" "Do they have access to transportation?" "Do family and friends know where they are and where they are going?"

Assessing risk also involves the professional noting and recording the patient's relevant issues and personal history. For example, have they previously attempted suicide, which makes them higher risk than if they have no previous attempts? Is there a family history of mental illness and suicide attempts? Often it is difficult to get this information together in a limited amount of time but the more that is known, the more accurate the risk assessment, and the more valuable it can be to professionals who might be able to help.

Finally, when assessing suicidal risk, the treating professional will need to know the relevant motives and any other risk factors that might be influencing the patient. Trying to determine the motivation behind their desire to die now, or during past attempts, can help identify the issues that are driving them to the brink of suicide, and can generate some options that could help to alleviate the crisis. The key is to know as many of the patient's risk factors as possible.

ASSESS CONDITION

Following the basic risk assessment, the next step is to complete the picture of a person's life and circumstances. The professional will want to know if the person is working, in school, retired, disabled, married, living alone, in or recently in the military, among others. What type of support system do they have? Are there any family members and friends who are particularly close to the patient and how often can they offer contact and support? In addition, knowing about any family issues or crises, or if there are any major problems involving their friends will be helpful. Are there any business, professional, legal, or financial problems that could be relevant? Finally, has the person in crisis ever experienced a traumatic situation or crisis such as a rape, assault, robbery, natural disaster, or major accident?

It is also vital to have a clear picture of other medical and/or mental health conditions for which the person is being treated. Knowing specific diagnoses and medication dosages is essential, as well as the seriousness of the symptoms they are experiencing, their response to treatment (improving or not), and their *prognosis* (the expected outcome of treatment).

Additional information about the problem(s) that the patient is facing will assist in determining the problem's acuity or chronicity: an *acute* problem has risen recently and becomes more intense at a faster rate, and may go away more quickly; a *chronic* problem has existed for a longer period of time, the severity tends to increase slowly, and usually takes a longer time to resolve (or may never improve). Understanding the acuity or chronicity of the problem(s) gives the treating professional data as to how long the person has been dealing with the issues in question, how severe the problems might be, and how likely they are to get better on their own or with treatment.

TREATMENTS

Following a suicide attempt an assessment must be done to determine which types of treatment are warranted and where treatment opportunities are available. When the attempt is first realized, there will be an acute phase of treatment that will focus on stabilizing the situation, treating immediate and/or life threatening conditions, and keeping the person safe. The first priority is to treat the symptoms and conditions that the person presents. If they are not breathing, cardiopulmonary resuscitation (CPR) should be started if it is medically possible and reasonable. If they have taken pills or poison, they should be rushed to a hospital or emergency treatment facility as soon as possible. If they are bleeding, it should be stopped or controlled. Immediate care for the presenting condition must be provided by an appropriate professional or help should be called as soon as possible.

After stabilizing the situation, the person must be kept as safe as possible and not allowed to leave. The person should not be dismissed and sent home even if they say they are now safe; they must be evaluated by a trained professional. Going to a hospital emergency room is usually a wise first step because the medical personnel can take responsibility for the patient. The person who is suicidal must be closely supervised by a responsible person until appropriate professional care is available.

Once the patient is stabilized, the next step is to determine the types of continuing treatment that will be most beneficial. Carefully controlled medications can be helpful if the person is upset and/or depressed. Giving a suicidal person a bottle of pills may put them at more risk than actually helping them. However, antidepressant medications typically take approximately a month to begin working, so medication is not usually a "quick fix" but must be part of a more comprehensive treatment plan. There are concerns that antidepressant medications may cause some patients to feel suicidal, which necessitates watching patients more closely. While this is a controversial issue, it is not generally an issue for patients who are being followed closely by their providers.

Other types of medical treatments can be useful with suicidal patients depending upon their condition and the seriousness of their attempt. Electroconvulsive therapy (ECT), sometimes called "electro-shock therapy" is occasionally prescribed for people who are so seriously depressed that they are not responding to medications or other therapies. As alarming as shock therapy may sound, it is not like what is presented in old movies. It is quite safe and offers the patient positive effects with very little risk. However, shock therapy is not a first-line treatment; it is only used if no other treatments are working or if the person is so high risk for suicide that it is too dangerous to wait for medications to take effect.

Hospitalization is another form of medical treatment and is warranted if a person is high risk for suicide and needs to be watched continuously for their safety. The advantage of in-hospital treatment is that medications in supervised settings can be used higher doses than if the person were outside the hospital. Higher doses mean that the medication can be increased to a therapeutic level quicker, thereby stabilizing the patient sooner. Usually a patient is in the hospital for only a few days or a couple of weeks at most. Not only do insurance companies refuse to pay for expensive in-patient treatment, but it is also usually in the best interest of the patient to get them quickly back into their own routine. Most hospitalizations are done voluntarily when the patient agrees to enter the hospital, but they can leave if they want to. People cannot be kept in the hospital against their will unless they are a "demonstrable risk to harm themselves or someone else." If a voluntary patient wants to leave the hospital, but the doctors and providers feel that they are too big a risk for suicide or for harming someone else, most states allow the hospital to keep the patient in a locked ward for 72 hours; afterward the hospital must release the patient or the hospital and provider must go to court to have them involuntarily committed to the hospital. In reality, most courts are reluctant to take away a person's rights, and involuntary commitment is not nearly as common as it used to be. Used appropriately, hospitalizing a suicidal patient is a dependable way to begin intensive treatment quickly and to keep them safe. Once stabilized, the patient is usually discharged to the continuing care with their own providers outside of the hospital, and if they do not have a provider, the hospital will usually find one and set up an appointment.

In addition to medical treatments, a variety of psychosocial treatments are available depending upon the underlying causes of the person's difficulties; when a diagnosis and treatment plan have been established, the patient's other conditions can be treated; for example, depression, schizophrenia, anxiety disorder, among others. Types of treatments include individual and group psychotherapy for the patient, as well as groups for relatives and friends of the patient. Some people might question how helpful "talk" therapy can be for someone who is suicidal. Psychotherapy can be very helpful and effective, but it is important to know that the two best predictors of psychotherapeutic success are the experience of the therapist and the motivation of the patient. Choosing a therapist who is licensed and appropriately trained is important, and the PCPs and/or the insurance companies can provide you with a list of providers. Ultimately, it is the patient who must develop a comfortable and trusting working relationship with the professional. The patient is advised to attend several therapy sessions before deciding if it is the right person or the right type of therapy. Jumping from one therapist to another is never helpful because the process is not given enough time to really make a difference.

Group therapy involves patients with similar issues attending sessions together under the leadership of a professional. In this setting people not only learn from the therapist but from one another as well. There are also therapy groups for family members or friends of those who have attempted or committed suicide. Finding an appropriate therapy group can be challenging, but medical providers, employee assistance programs, hospitals, churches, insurance companies, as well as local, regional, state, or national professional societies can all be found on line or in a telephone directory, and these sources can usually provide names of professionals who provide the services that are needed.

Support groups for family and friends are similar to therapy groups in that involve several people with specific problems or concerns, such as dealing with a loved one who attempted or committed suicide. While survivors of suicide attempts and those who are high risk for suicide should be treated by professionals with experience, support groups are helpful for sharing with and listening to people who have "walked in your shoes." Patients who are being treated professionally may benefit from a support group but only *if it is recommended by the professional who is treating them.* Support groups are typically not run by professionals and are usually free or have a small voluntary donation that is optional.

Family therapy is sometimes recommended for survivors of suicide attempts and their family members. The family unit will work with a professional therapist who helps deal with the suicide attempt and the family issues that may have been related to the attempt or may have surfaced following the attempt. This type of treatment is not intended to "blame" the family, but rather to discuss some of the frightening, upsetting, and anger-filled emotions that exist. Identifying those family members who hold considerable influence on its members can be important to sorting out the complexities of suicide.

Finally, in-hospital care usually involves psychosocial treatments as well, and is conducted by trained professionals who can involve a full range of therapies: individual, group, or family. Sometimes inpatient treatment will involve art therapy, music therapy, dance therapy, scholastic help, and tutoring.

Summary

This chapter addressed issues of prevention and treatment for suicidality, all complex issues often requiring many options and approaches. Although all suicide attempts will never be prevented, knowing what to look for and what treatment options are available for those at risk will help to reduce the frequency.

Section II

Contemporary Controversies and Issues

CHAPTER 6

Mental Health, Mental Illness, and Suicide

Is Suicide "Crazy"?

Behavior that is considered dramatic and "abnormal" can be anything from wild and harmful to thrilling and dangerous. The label "crazy" can be used for unusual behaviors as well as for "crazy movies" such as *Jackass* and for "crazy" activities such as the X Games. Since it can be used in either a positive or negative context, it makes sense to stay away from terms such as "crazy" when describing someone who is experiencing difficulties psychologically or emotionally.

While it is reasonable to avoid terms such as "crazy" that might have many different meanings, it is still a legitimate point to try to determine if someone who thinks about or attempts suicide is psychologically or emotionally troubled or suffers from a diagnosed mental condition. As mentioned earlier, there are certainly psychological conditions that make it more likely that someone will think about or attempt suicide—for example, mood disorders such as depression and bipolar disorder, but also serious mental conditions such as schizophrenia make a person higher risk for suicide. To be diagnosed with any mental condition means that the person shows certain *symptoms* (including such things as unusual behavior, thoughts, or feelings) that would qualify them for a specific diagnosis. However, from a practical standpoint, a "clinical" or actual psychological condition that would be diagnosed and treated will usually have several characteristics. For example, it usually involves symptoms that create problems for the person in question because these symptoms can either make them feel uncomfortable (for example, anxiety or depression), or by creating difficult situations for them with other people or with society. The other main thing we look at in determining whether or not a person is suffering from a mental disorder is the extent to which their condition interferes with their normal functioning at work or school, interpersonally, socially, medically, or in other major areas of their life.

We know that some mental health conditions do make a person more likely to attempt suicide, but that does not mean that *every* person who attempts suicide suffers from a diagnosed mental disorder. At different points in this book we have referred to conditions that might lead a person to attempt suicide that might seem very rational on the surface—for example, having an incurable and very painful disease that will only get worse; under these conditions someone might elect to end their life rather than continue to suffer. Even if people did not agree with this decision, most would at least understand it. A spy or soldier might kill themselves rather than be captured and tortured and particularly if they had some very important but highly secret information—this type of suicide would probably be looked at as heroic by many or even most people. These are two very extreme examples, but do point out that there might be cases where a person's decision to end their own life might not be the result of a mental disorder, but rather the result of a conscious decision based on rational and understandable circumstances.

In summary then, a person might be diagnosed with a mental condition if they had symptoms that cause them distress or which create difficulties for them, and when these symptoms interfere with their ability to function normally in the important areas of his or her life. Of course it is also true that in most disorders the symptoms have to exist for more than just a brief instance—they usually occur over time and in different situations as well.

It is not difficult to see how a person with serious psychological problems might be at higher risk for suicide, but it is more difficult to imagine how a person who is very psychologically healthy might get to the point of killing themselves. The best way to look at this is to accept the fact that a person who is emotionally fragile and who does not have much strength to draw on might see suicide as the only option for them. In this case, however, the decision to commit suicide is more of a reflection of their mental state than the circumstances they find themselves in. Too often when people attempt suicide and talk about the things that "drove" them to it others will say or think things like, "Why kill yourself? It wasn't that bad." Or, "If they had only waited it would have worked out ok." In other words, people would often think that the circumstances that were the apparent reason for the attempted suicide were not severe enough to warrant death.

On the other hand, if a person who is very psychologically healthy were to attempt suicide it would more likely be due to an extreme situation that was unavoidable, would not improve, and had serious or catastrophic results. For example, situations such as a person killing themselves to avoid an awful and horrific death from a terrible and incurable disease, or the spy with state secrets killing themselves to prevent a war that would kill millions of people, would be understandable. Thus, the healthier a person is, the more of an extreme situation it would take for them to attempt suicide. All of us might wonder what it would take for us to try to kill ourselves, but in all probability the extreme situations that might result in suicide would be so unlikely as to be nearly impossible for the huge majority of people. However, we are still left with the minority of people for whom suicide is a real risk, and to ignore them is not acceptable. We may never be able to prevent all suicides, but by learning and understanding more about it we have a chance to prevent some of them—one suicide prevented is one life saved and a future preserved.

If mental illness makes a person more vulnerable to suicidal risk, it is important to understand exactly what it is about these conditions that make a person want to kill themselves. Of course that depends in part on the type of disorder that they have and the symptoms that they experience. If a person is suffering from a mood disorder where their feelings are distorted and disruptive, then this will affect how they feel, act, and think. For example, when a person is depressed they feel negatively about almost everything and feel like it will never get better and never end (helplessness and hopelessness). Further, the depressed person feels badly about themselves and may even feel like they deserve to die. When depressed, people also interpret most of their life experiences in a negative way and seem unable to experience any pleasure or anything positive at all.

Anxiety disorders are similar in that the symptoms that people experience are so unpleasant that people may get to the point where they feel that they cannot continue to live feeling as badly as they do. It is also a complicating factor that it is fairly common that people with anxiety disorders will also have depression as a secondary problem and of course having both types of disorders would heighten the suicidal risk.

In psychotic disorders such as schizophrenia, the person's thinking, emotions, and behavior are seriously disturbed and often their ability to control their impulses is compromised. Thus, in these types of disorders a person might commit suicide because of some bizarre idea that most of the rest of us would not be able to comprehend or understand. For example, a psychotic person might believe that they are the rebirth of Jesus Christ and kill themselves to prepare for a second reincarnation. Another thing that

Often, people who might be helped do not have access to the kind of care that might make a difference. (Monkey Business Images/Dreamstime.com)

sometimes happens with psychotic individuals is that if they actually start thinking more normally they may decide that they would rather die than live with a serious mental illness for the rest of their life.

Although there are an infinite number of reasons why a person with a mental illness might attempt suicide it usually boils down to disturbed thinking and poor impulse control. Obviously their emotions are very important too, but they are important primarily because of the ways that they make people think and act. When people feel that their life is miserable and will only get worse it is easy to understand why they might want to end their life, but what they do not fully understand is that their assessment of their life and circumstances is not accurate and is based on a mental abnormality and not on reality—of course just pointing that out to them is never an adequate solution for a suicidal person because they just think that you do not fully understand what they are experiencing. If we add poor impulse control to the disturbed thinking, it would then make it more likely that the patient would not be able (or even want to) control and inhibit the suicidality.

Another way to approach the issue of mental illness and suicidality is to look at the reasons why people who are psychologically healthy are less likely to attempt and commit suicide. It seems obvious that happier and healthier people are less likely to want to kill themselves, but more importantly, why is that? What is it about being psychologically healthy that makes a person more resilient and less vulnerable to suicidality? Reviewing the characteristics of healthy people should make this clearer.

- Effective—the person who is effective not only has better control of their lives and environment, but they are also less likely to feel overwhelmed and helpless. They also are more likely to engage in activities that they enjoy and get pleasure from.
- Efficient—this means that the person gets the things done that need to get done and also helps them from feeling overwhelmed. Further, by being efficient they have time to relax and to do other things that they like to do.
- Appropriate—when people behave inappropriately others typically try to avoid them because they are too uncomfortable to be around. When people behave appropriately it is likely that others will want to be around them, enjoy their company, provide support, and share in pleasurable activities.
- Flexible—people who are flexible can adapt to changes in their environment and circumstances without feeling overwhelmed. They rarely feel "trapped" because they always seem able to find another way to solve the problem. They also seem to be more creative in finding approaches to problems and find novel solutions to difficult situations.
- Can profit from experience—I have often told my own children, "Everyone makes mistakes, but smart people only make a particular mistake once." Being able to make mistakes, learn from them, and do better the next time is very important to maintaining psychological health and resisting the awful feelings that lead people to suicide. Where people often get into trouble is when they keep doing the same thing, get the same negative outcome, and then do the same thing again. An old Chinese proverb states, "He who performs the same act expecting a different outcome is a fool." Another way to think about this was told to me by a patient who is also in Alcoholics Anonymous; he said, "If nothing changes—nothing changes." There is some real wisdom in those two quotes.
- Interpersonally effective—enjoying and being comfortable with others is very important. It gives us social support when we are feeling down, but also gives us different perspectives and options to deal with issues that face us. When we are close to others we also have opportunities to provide help and support them as well, and this

usually makes us feel better for being a good friend, and also helps us remember that there are many things that can be done to help someone deal with a challenging situation.

* Self-secure—people who truly know and accept themselves are usually happier and deal with stress more effectively. Understanding and accepting our faults but trying to improve them is very healthy and is also something that helps prevent those feelings of helplessness and hopelessness. If you know, accept, and care for yourself, you are not likely to want to kill yourself.

It is very important to understand that suicide might possibly be the result of someone having a mental illness, but it is also true that not everyone who commits suicide is mentally ill and it is definitely true that the huge majority of people with mental conditions never attempt suicide. However, we do need to remember that since suicide could be a higher risk for some people with mental conditions, it is even more important that we try to make sure that people with psychological difficulties have access to appropriate care—not only is this just the right, smartest, and most cost-effective thing to do, but it also might save lives by reducing one of the risk factors for someone attempting suicide.

Similarly, by studying and understanding some of the things that contribute to people being more psychologically healthy, we can also understand what kinds of things we should foster and strive for in order to protect people and ourselves from being more at risk for suicide. It makes good sense physically that if we exercise and take better care of our health then we are more likely to avoid illness and live longer and healthier lives. The same logic applies to mental health; the more people try to take care of themselves psychologically the more likely they are to live happier and more productive lives and the less likely they are to commit suicide as the result of some treatable mental condition.

SUICIDE AND TREATMENT

Earlier in this book the topic of "prevention" was discussed in some detail, and the different things that could help to reduce the number of people who attempt and commit suicide were explored. However, it is also important to look at what medical and mental health providers can do to deal more effectively with suicidality. Rarely at the primary care level do providers inquire about things like depression or suicide, and even when depression is explored it is not likely that the provider will delve into the issue of suicide in any depth at all. In all fairness to the primary care providers, however, the patient is rarely at an appointment for the reasons of suicide or depression, and since the primary care provider is trying to see patients responsively (to treat what they come in for), they also need to treat people efficiently (to get everyone seen without undue waiting). What this means is that the provider may not get around to inquiring in depth about things like depression or suicide because it is not obvious that these might be issues, and they may not have to time to explore other issues.

It might seem unusual that a primary care provider might consider something like suicide when looking at the care and treatment needs of a patient in routine primary care. However, if the patient's history suggests mental health issues then this should always be a topic that the provider keeps in mind—this must be assessed and updated even if only briefly. If the patient has a history of suicidality then the primary care provider should keep an eye and ear open to determine if this is an issue that needs further attention or a referral. Thus, from a primary care perspective, continuing care for suicidality probably means that the provider will always keep this in mind as something that needs to be assessed and possibly followed or referred out if it looks like a serious problem.

In most training programs for doctors, nurses, physician's assistants, and nurse practitioners the training today is much better to help them understand, recognize, and respond to psychological issues like suicidality. One of the things that keep many providers from looking into these issues is that they are unsure what to do if they find something questionable or concerning—this is where better training and awareness come in. At the primary care level it is not likely that fully appropriate treatment will be available to meet all of the mental health needs that a patient presents. In some very forward-thinking primary care offices there may actually be a psychologist and psychiatrist available for patients who need to be evaluated and possibly referred for further treatment. In addition, there may also be social workers or counselors who can help as well. Even in these types of offices, however, it is rare that the mental health providers will do more than assess the condition, meet the patient for a few visits for simple types of problems, and then refer them out for more in-depth treatment. Probably the best thing that can be done in the primary care setting is to adequately assess which patients need to be referred for further evaluation and possible treatment. Clearly, to even assess and refer, the right questions have to be asked and the provider needs to know how to interpret and understand the responses of a person who needs further treatment for a mental health condition.

If the determination is made to refer a patient for mental health treatment because they appear to be a suicide risk, it is important that they be referred to an appropriate provider who has the credentials, skills, and experience necessary to deal with these types of complex and serious issues. There are a wide variety of different types of treatment that can be helpful to a person experiencing a psychological problem, but it is essential to get a person to the right type of provider. If medication is warranted, then referring a patient to a psychiatrist or other licensed provider who is trained to prescribe psychotropic drugs (psychiatric medications) is essential. If psychotherapeutic treatment is considered to be appropriate, then a referral needs to be made to a licensed and trained provider who has the training, skills, and experience necessary to deal with the particular type of problem that the patient presents. Suicide is a very complex and serious problem that requires that a provider knows what they are doing and has dealt with this type of issue many times before. When a provider is learning to deal with something like suicide they must have the proper training and education, but then they must also have supervised experience where they are trained and observed so that they do not make critical mistakes in treatment that might have serious consequences.

Suicidal patients usually have a number of other issues that they are dealing with and often these issues involve some of the things that have brought them to the point of suicide. Clearly, one of the things that we try to do when dealing with suicidal patients is to help them work though some of the things that they feel are causing them to want to kill themselves. Since patients who are in suicidal crisis typically feel like there is nothing that can be done to help them with the problems they are facing the first thing that the mental health professional will usually try to do is to start creating options and try to "buy some time" to get past the immediate crisis. Saying things like, "You tell me that there is nothing that can help you and there is no reason to keep living, but I am not sure that you have looked into all of the things that might actually help. Before you do something so final as suicide, maybe we should make certain that there are not some other alternatives that could actually make a difference," may actually give them reason to think and perhaps even question their decision. Also saying things like, "If you are feeling that you are not safe, let's look at some options to keep you safe while you consider some other things that might actually help," respects how they feel, indicates the professional's concern and support, and keeps the choices in the person's hands.

There might be times when a professional might actually need to have a person hospitalized because they are so acutely at risk that it is unlikely that they will be able or willing to take steps to keep themselves safe. When this happens the professional needs to do whatever is needed to protect the patient, and if that upsets the patient so much they do not want to come back to see that provider, at least they are still alive to be able to make that choice. In my personal experience, when I have felt that a patient needs to be in the hospital and I tell them this but make it their choice, with some reassurance that they will not be hospitalized for very long (a few days usually), they almost always agree to enter the hospital voluntarily. However, if they are not willing to take that step I would call the police or crisis team if I truly thought the person's life was at risk.

When trying to sort through the issues confronting a suicidal patient it is never helpful to tell a person that their issues, "aren't really that bad, and certainly nothing worth killing yourself over." For most suicidal patients, the way they feel makes suicide seem like a reasonable option, and telling them the problems are not that bad only confirms their suspicion that you have no idea how they actually feel. I also tell the people I train that you *never* tell a patient, "I know how you feel," unless you have had the exact problem that they are facing; once again, this just confirms that you do not know what you are talking about.

Starting to identify issues, looking at logical options, and developing strategies for dealing with those problems is usually a good way to begin working with patients who are potentially suicidal. However, there are also some other approaches that can be helpful. For example, some will use a technique called the "suicide contract." When I use this technique I will typically make an agreement like, "If you get to a point where you feel unsafe and are afraid you are going to harm yourself, our agreement is that you will not do anything unless you call me first, and you agree to wait to do something harmful until you have heard from me. My part of the contract is that I will call you back as soon as I can, will help you identify the particular crises, and also help you generate some ways to deal with them. I will agree not to 'panic' and call the authorities and will just help defuse the situation. If I think your life is at risk I will not do anything without telling you first." This approach can work very well with the right kind of patient or client, but for some it would not be helpful—I usually find that being honest with patients and telling them your ideas gives them a chance to think about them and reject them if they choose to. However, if I have a patient who is reluctant to make a suicide contract I will also tell them that if I think they are at risk then since I am not bound by the contract either; then I will feel free to contact the authorities with or without their knowledge.

Although there are many techniques that mental health providers learn to use to deal with and hopefully defuse suicidal crises, I think there are a basic few things that always seem to be part of a good strategy. First, you must listen and listen carefully; never assume you know what a person is thinking, but try to hear and understand what their concerns and issues are and what seems to be blocking them from finding a solution other than suicide. Second, you must be honest and trustworthy—never go back on your word or try to "trick" them into something you have not discussed with them. Third, try to see things from their perspective (even if it is distorted), and let them know you understand—even if you do not agree with them. Finally, know what your options are—the resources that can help you, the people and institutions you can access for help or support, and any other things that might be of value in the situation. For professionals dealing with suicidal crises, these basic principles can be very helpful and might even save a life.

Role and Responsibility of the Treating Professional

One of the most difficult messages that I provide to mental health providers who I am training is that if someone truly wants to kill themselves there is probably not much you can do about it. Buying time, looking for options, using therapeutic strategies, helping defuse a crisis—these are all things that can be done and often are very helpful. However, one of the most difficult things for a professional who is trained to help people is the realization that there will be people who you just cannot help regardless of how hard you try, how well trained and experienced you are, and how badly you want to help them. Some people may simply be beyond help, and that is not a criticism of the professional but sometimes just a reality.

Treating suicidal patients is very difficult and demanding work, and you are always concerned that you might have not done the right things or perhaps you could have done more. However, to truly be effective in dealing with high-risk patients one has to accept the situation as it exists, deal with it the best way that you can, and then step away. The professional can never put themselves in the role of the "rescuer" or "savior." Neither of these roles is helpful or even consistent with the role of provider. As soon as the provider puts themselves in the roles of saving someone's life and keeping them alive at all costs, they then lose their professional objectivity and can no longer function as a professional who is trying to treat the patient. This also opens the provider up to the possibility of being manipulated by the patient who will use this as a way of making the provider do what the patient wants rather than what is the best treatment. Of course, I am not saying that the provider should not care about keeping the patient alive, or that it should not matter to them if the patient kills themselves—to be effective you have to care and care deeply, but you just cannot let the caring get in the way of good professional treatment of the patient.

In treating the suicidal patient, the role of the provider is that of the well trained, concerned, and competent professional. The responsibility of the provider is to deliver the best and most competent and responsive care to the patient that the provider is capable of.

SUMMARY

In this chapter, the issue of mental illness and suicidality was discussed in more depth. The conclusion is that mental illness is one of the significant risk factors for suicidality. It is also true that there are some forms of mental illness that are higher risk for suicide than others. However, it must also be remembered that not all people who attempt or commit suicide are mentally ill. Similarly, we also need to recall that the huge majority of people with various forms of psychological problems never attempt or commit suicide.

Some of the therapeutic issues faced in dealing with suicidal patients were explored and the role and responsibilities of treating professionals were discussed as well. Not only is suicide a very complex and often puzzling issue, but the treatment of the suicidal patient is also very complex and difficult and requires that the treating professional have a clear understanding of their role and responsibility in dealing with patients who may be suicidal.

CHAPTER 7

Patient Rights and the Right to Die

INTRODUCTION

In recent years there has been considerable interest in defining and protecting the rights of patients. Doctors, professors, authors, and medical ethicists (people who study and research issues involving the ethics of medicine) debate these issues and have been instrumental in identifying patients' concerns and clarifying the quality of care patients and families can and should expect from their medical care providers. Some of the basic rights of patients include:

1. Patients have the right to informed consent regarding treatment decisions, appropriate and timely access to care from specialists, and to have their privacy and confidentiality protected. This means that patients must be informed of treatment decisions and be allowed to consent or to refuse treatment. If a patient is incapable of making a decision about their treatment, they have the right to sign a "Living Will," which gives instructions about their future care and usually identifies a "Health Care Proxy," who is someone chosen by the patient to make medical decisions on the patient's behalf if they are not able to do so. Patients also have the right to pursue specialty care when appropriate, and to have their records and medical/personal information protected from unwarranted and unnecessary access by others. A patient must sign a form that gives a provider or company permission to release their personal information to another specific person or company. This release can identify specific dates or procedures

or can include all available information; it can also indicate when the release is to terminate, after a one time use or after a specific date.

2. Patients have the right to concise and easily understood information about their condition and their treatments, and to have this information made available to them when they need or want to make decisions about their care. They also have the right to specify those people with whom their medical information can be shared.

3. Patients have the right to know which available treatments will be covered by insurance and what they or their family will be financially responsible for.

4. Patients have the right to know what their options are in terms of selecting providers, and to have useful information about those options and the available providers, as well as the costs for prospective treatments. They also have the right to know if providers are receiving incentives for specific practice patterns; that is, do the providers receive benefits for offering one form of treatment over another.

5. Patients have the right to access appropriate treatment options as well as the right to choose options that are medically reasonable. Further, they also have the right to refuse treatment if they are competent to make that decision. Competence implies that the patient is physically and mentally capable of exercising reasonable judgment in making choices about their care; competence is a legal term that is based on a court ruling that determines a person's ability to make decisions for themselves.

6. Patients have the right to decline treatment, which also suggests that patients have the right to choose to die if their condition is hopeless, if there are no reasonable treatment options, and if they are in considerable pain and/or discomfort. This last right is still controversial and is the subject of much debate.

While it is vitally important that patients and their representatives know of their rights and how to protect and exercise those rights, it is equally important for patients and families to recognize the patient's responsibilities, especially when considering a patient's right to die. Specifically, a patient must present evidence of being competent to make their own decisions and that they are responsible about the course of their life and their treatment. According to the National Health Council Board of Directors, responsibilities of a capable patient include:

1. The patient actively pursues a healthy lifestyle by making healthy choices about their behavior and their life.
2. The patient actively participates in making decisions about their health care by being an involved member of the treatment team in order to make their own preferences and reasons known and clear.
3. The patient becomes knowledgeable about their health plan; if pursuing treatment options, patient and family asks for information from their insurance or managed care company in order to be aware of what insurance will pay for and what they will be responsible for themselves; it is not up to medical providers to educate patients about their insurance or coverage.
4. The patient cooperates with courses of treatment that have been mutually agreed upon by the patient, family, and providers. If a patient changes their mind about a course of treatment, it is the responsibility of the patient to inform the providers and to discuss revising the treatment plan.

While considering a patient's rights and responsibilities, the issue of a patient's right to commit suicide, or to die, becomes critical. Usually a patient's right to die means that they have the right to refuse treatment or to refuse food and water in order to die from the discontinuation of life-sustaining actions. Some people believe that a patient's right to make a life-ending choice should logically include the right to call upon someone whom they trust to assist them with taking active steps toward death. Clearly, these considerations only apply in situations where the potential suicide is a medical patient who has decided that they want to end their life rather than continue to live with their disease. The considerations are not appropriate, for example, for a person who is impaired by drugs or alcohol or who is personally distraught by a tragedy or other trauma. In order to fully address issues such as the right to die, all factors that are relevant to the situation must be carefully evaluated prior to making the decision to live or die. This issue of a patient's rights is still quite controversial, and there are no generally accepted standards that are universally applied.

THE RIGHT TO DIE

Throughout recorded history debates have endured about the right to die and the right to commit suicide. Typically, the right to die is less controversial, and yet this right is still complex and sometimes confusing. The issues regarding the right to commit suicide are often debated from various points of view, which can cause even more confusion. Some arguments are legal, political, religious, spiritual, or philosophical, and many are individual and very personal. As mentioned in an earlier chapter, the historical aspects of suicide were often based on religious views, which typically rely on assumptions such as, "God gave you life; only God has the right to take it," or on the belief that only the state could give approval for suicide. Thus, these two assumptions show the conflict between the rights of the individual and the rights of God or the state.

Recently, several countries that have struggled with right-to-die issues have composed guidelines for euthanasia that reflect the culture of their country, as well as their attitudes about death and freedom of choice. Euthanasia refers to facilitating the death of another person—usually for humanitarian reasons. Voluntary euthanasia means that a patient chooses someone else to assist with their suicide because the patient is unable to take the action themselves. As of 2009 some forms of voluntary euthanasia were deemed legal in Belgium, Luxembourg, the Netherlands, Switzerland, and in the U.S. states of Oregon and Washington (Montana and Vermont will allow assisted suicide in specific situations as well).

The Netherlands was one of the first countries in the world to legalize voluntary euthanasia in 2001. However, this law only applies to situations where the patient's case is "hopeless and unbearable." If a person helps another commit suicide, and those specific conditions are not met, the act is considered illegal and the person could be charged with a crime. In 2010, in the Netherlands, a group of people started an initiative called *Uit Vrije Wil* (out of free will) that has the support of many prominent people from different backgrounds, including physicians, scholars, philosophers, clergy, lawyers, artists and writers, as well as many average citizens. They have asked for a new law to state that any person over the age of 70 who feels tired of life and does not want to live any longer should be allowed the option of voluntary euthanasia even if they have the capacity to kill themselves. This group also insists on the right to die with dignity in a manner that is painless and easy and can be facilitated by a physician or another person who has the knowledge and means to end the person's life.

Closer to home, Canada and the United States continue to struggle with issues such as euthanasia and the right to die. Recently, in 2011, a Canadian Supreme Court judge was requested to speed up a right-to-die lawsuit so that a patient with ALS (Lou Gehrig's disease) could commit suicide with a doctor's assistance; this did not happen and she died of an infection in 2012. In British Columbia, Canada, a civil liberties lawsuit representing six patients and families is challenging those Canadian laws that make it a criminal offense to aid seriously ill individuals in committing suicide. In the United States, if a physician or other person gives a shot to a patient who wants to die from a lethal injection, it is considered illegal in every state; however, as mentioned earlier, a third party, or someone other than the medical professional, can give a patient the means (e.g., drugs) to end their own life in Washington, Oregon, Montana, and Vermont. However, there must be clear confirmation that the patient is of sound mind when requesting suicide and that the patient is suffering from a terminal illness. This confirmation must be attested to by a doctor and other witnesses.

The concept of euthanasia may seem reasonable to those who would consider it, but many people completely disagree and feel that suicide under any circumstances is wrong and that assisted suicide is just murder. Also, there are many who are concerned that laws, allowing for assisted suicide or euthanasia in the patient's "best interests" but without their consent, are open to abuse and misuse. For example, someone could "talk" a patient into committing suicide in order to gain their inheritance sooner, or a government official or insurance company executive could encourage a physician to help a patient "commit suicide" because the incurable disease was very expensive to treat. Many people, including doctors, legal scholars, and patient-rights' advocates, are aware of and concerned about the potential risks and abuses of laws permitting medically assisted suicide, and that is one of the reasons why these laws are still very controversial.

Many feel that people have the right to determine how and when they are going to die. (AP Photo/Don Ryan)

In trying to apply legal remedies to these difficult moral and ethical issues, the laws must deal with two related but very different issues: first, there are laws that *grant permission* to a person to aid another in committing suicide, and there are laws *banning harm* to patients in order to prevent a form of homicide. There are new laws against *causing premature death* that try to protect patients while giving them the freedom to choose how and when they die. These laws also offer some protection for those who assist in a suicide and should not be considered an accomplice to a homicide in the traditional sense.

In states where right-to-death laws exist, the laws typically grant permission to use life-ending chemicals as a way of bringing the patient's life to a peaceful and painless end. However, there are always safeguards and procedures that must be followed. First, the doctor must certify that the patient is qualified and meets the guidelines specified in the law. Second, the required waiting period must be observed to make sure that the patient does not change their mind. Third, the physician will write a prescription for life-ending chemicals (drugs), but the laws do not state when or how the patient should take the chemicals that will cause immediate death; this part of the process is left entirely in the patient's hands.

While the laws in the Netherlands have occasionally changed, in the past it was possible for a patient to ask for euthanasia to end their suffering and for the physician to inject them with life-ending chemicals if the doctor found that the patient met the legal criteria qualifying them for this procedure. Recently, however, physicians have opted to increase the patient's pain medications or other drugs leading to terminal sedation; this method is helpful and humane, and does not require the reams of legal paperwork that are required for a lethal injection.

Another legal approach that is being discussed, but is not fully operational, is a law prohibiting the act of "causing premature death." A law like this will most likely be included with laws dealing with homicide, as a low (or lowest) form of homicide rather than dealing with issues such as "assisted suicide." This law would place the burden of proof on the prosecution to prove that the death was in fact premature, not whether or not the act of the defendant caused the death. It would also offer the additional protection that the defendant was "innocent until proven guilty." Further, the final judgment would be in the hands of a jury, which would be responsible for deciding if the actual death was premature or not—if the patient was about to die anyway then it would not be premature. This type of law would allow the apprehension of people sometimes called the "Angels of Death," who are self-appointed perpetrators of "mercy killings" who feel that the patient no longer has a meaningful quality of life and who have acted without the expressed wishes of the patient or family. This type of law against causing premature death would also need to address the prevention of "irrational" suicide in instances in which the patient is not competent or capable of making the judgment to end their life.

Legal protections must be carefully considered and crafted in ways that will protect patient rights first but will also protect the person(s) who are carrying out the wishes of a patient in legal and ethical ways, including suicide. The introduction of new laws that will help to prevent unwanted acts of "premature death" offers a new way of protecting a patient's right to die with dignity, but it will be some time before the issues involved in this type of law are finally worked out. As technologies change and medical ethics continues to evolve and become clearer, the laws in the future will also need to change to meet new standards and cultural considerations.

SOME OTHER ETHICAL ISSUES IN THE RIGHT TO DIE

The right to die is an ethical or institutional entitlement that permits a person to commit suicide or to undergo voluntary euthanasia, assuming that they have a terminal illness and that they possess the capacity and competence to make that decision. It sanctions a person's right to commit suicide, to receive assisted suicide, or to end life-sustaining treatment if continuing their life would be filled with suffering and their death would occur naturally within a relatively short time. The legal/ethical question of who, if anyone, should have the right to make these decisions is the core issue in this type of law.

In countries where debates have occurred and a consensus has been reached, the fundamental right to die encompasses the ideas that a person's body and life is their own and that they alone have the right to make decisions about how to end their life, if they are rational and competent to do so and without the undue influence of others. Thus, the person's decision must not be effected by conditions of "mental illness" and/or by others who have "talked them into it."

In many countries, it is impossible for debates regarding the right to die to be conducted independent of the predominant religion of the culture. Hinduism, for example, accepts the right to die for those suffering terminal and painful conditions, but also for those who have no interest or desire to continue living and who have no responsibilities that need to be fulfilled. They allow for suicide through nonviolent methods such as fasting to the point of starvation (Prayopayesa), which is similar to what Jainism, a religion practiced mainly in India, permits, where people starve themselves to death if their quality of life and health is compromised to the point that they no longer want to live (Santhara). These fairly permissive spiritual views differ from many other religions that hold a much more severe attitude regarding suicide. In the Catholic faith, for example, suicide is considered to be a mortal sin that would keep a person from receiving the last rites and the blessings of the Church, forbidding them from being buried in a consecrated cemetery and from entering heaven.

In discussing issues involving the right to die, including permission to commit suicide, a distinction must be made between assisting a person to commit suicide and aiding them in the natural process of dying. Suicide means that the person wants to cease their existence and wants "leave this world"; the intent is the "self-destruction of personhood." This is very different from a person who feels that they have lived a wonderful and productive life, and now their time has come to an end. This very subtle difference is based on the "intention" of the act. What is the person actually trying to accomplish and why? What type of evidence is available to determine if the act of intentionally ending a person's life was legally and ethically permissible, and not just be based on the fanciest, descriptive language?

Many have raised the question, "Can suicide ever be a truly rational choice?" Since the will to live is naturally present in human beings, some assert that choosing to go against one of the most powerful drives in humankind—the need to survive—is anything but "rational." Considerations that can help clarify the distinction between "irrational suicide" and voluntary death include:

1. Irrational suicide is harmful and voluntary death is helpful if it is judged by the outcome or the expected outcome. If harm comes to the patient without helpful benefit, it would be considered an irrational suicide.

2. Irrational suicide is "irrational" and voluntary death is rational, a somewhat confusing standard. "Irrational" suicide means that the resulting death does not seem to fit the apparent "causes" or reasons and does not seem to make sense to others; a voluntary death makes sense to most people and appears rational and logical under the circumstances. Irrational suicide is usually found to be impulsive, careless, while voluntary death is well planned.

3. Irrational suicide is considered to be regrettable and voluntary death is seen as admirable. If those who are left behind experience deep feelings of regret, it is more likely that the suicide was irrational. If, however, family and friends feel a sense of admiration,

mixed with sadness and relief, that the person ended their misery by choice by dying peacefully and "courageously," then the death would be considered voluntary.

It is important to note that the difference between irrational suicide and voluntary death is not just a change in vocabulary while describing the same thing. It is two very different outcomes resulting from qualitatively different acts. Thus, an irrational suicide is harmful to the patient, irrational, capricious, and regrettable. Conversely, a voluntary death is helpful to the patient, rational, well planned, and admirable.

OTHER RIGHT-TO-DIE ISSUES

There will never be unanimous agreement on a patient's right to die. Opinions on the many issues will vary and will continuously be debated as people and cultures change. While society has the right to pass laws permitting or preventing people from ending their lives, the decision to commit suicide is ultimately a personal choice that lies with the individual. Taking action to keep someone alive against their will, even if that person is conscious and clear-minded enough to make the decision to end their life, is in keeping with the beliefs and values of some that life is precious and no one must be allowed to destroy it under any circumstances. Others feel that the patient has the right to decide when they no longer want to continue living under certain circumstances and the right to take steps to die naturally and normally. Still others hold religious beliefs that only God has the right to give and take life away.

Society also has the right to establish acceptable standards for the protection of life and individual freedoms of those who are committed to helping a terminally ill person. Although patient rights are of most importance, it does not mean that families and friends do not have some protections of their own in these difficult situations. If a critically ill patient who is nearing death wants to live as long as their condition permits, caregivers may question whether the patient is conscious and capable enough to be able to make that decision to continue living in pain or to receive assistance in the form of medication to end life. Some will argue that we decide to humanely put our pets out of their misery, so why not do the same for people? Of course, people are not pets, and they possess the ability and the right to continue to receive life-sustaining treatment as long as possible. If the patient is mentally competent and understands the choices that have been presented to them, should they not have the right to choose to end a hopeless and painful life just as they would choose to continue to fight for life? If a patient is incapable of making a life-ending decision, a caregiver must be allowed to present proof of the patient's wishes with the full protection of the law.

SUMMARY

Clearly, when a person attempts and/or commits suicide not only is their own life impacted or ended, the lives of many other people are affected as well. Questions and feelings about motives and guilt can affect a survivor's life significantly and permanently. It is important to remember that if someone is determined to die, it is not always possible to protect them from themselves, and that sometimes the completion of the suicidal act can be accidental. Although family and friends do not have rights regarding the patient, unless they are a minor, they can make suggestions for treatment or hospitalization and most importantly can call 911 or another adult to help with a crisis situation. One can never control the thoughts, feelings, or behaviors of another, but you can certainly control the things that you do, and that will sometimes include "backing off" when your actions become ineffective.

In the organization AlAnon (support groups for those who have friends/family dealing with addictive disease), members discuss the importance of "detaching with love," that is the act of stepping away from someone you care about and who is deeply troubled, as with a suicidal person, and allowing the person to experience the results of their own actions. It may also mean letting someone else, such as a professional or a relative, take over the situation and do what is in the patient's best interests, a most difficult decision to make. It does not mean one stops caring or worrying; it means protecting oneself while helping someone in crisis.

This observation is not intended to be negative or fatalistic, but rather hopeful and realistic. Being realistic about what can be done for someone intent on committing suicide and avoiding the trap of being manipulated into making a situation worse and more dangerous is the healthiest and most helpful action that can be taken. If you take reasonable steps to keep a vulnerable person safe, notify a responsible person of the situation and then step away, you are placing the person's life back in their own hands where it belongs, which will hopefully result in in them taking positive actions toward getting the help that they need. Offering to help, suggesting treatment, offering to drive the person to the hospital, or even just informing a responsible person about your concerns can make a difference, but sometimes none of these are enough to stop someone from attempting or committing suicide. As tragic as this is, sometimes there is nothing that anyone could have done to make a difference, a difficult concept to accept.

CHAPTER 8

Roles of Family, Friends, Professionals, Society, and the Law

Anyone who is close to a friend or family member who commits suicide knows how traumatic it is and how it permanently affects all of the survivors. A suicide also impacts society and the professionals who play a role in its prevention and treatment. This chapter examines in more depth the roles and the steps that can be taken to identify and deal with individuals who are struggling with issues of self-harm or suicide.

ROLES OF FAMILY AND FRIENDS

Few things are more frightening than to realize that someone close to you is at risk for killing themselves and that you have no idea what to do. "What if I do the wrong thing?" "What if I don't do enough?" Basically, if a person is suicidal, you can point out alternatives, show that you care, and get a doctor or psychologist involved as soon as possible. As mentioned earlier, you should never put yourself in the position of being the only one that can keep the person alive, nor should you do nothing. It is important to be aware of some of the warning signs of suicide and know how to respond if you notice any of them.

The major warning signs of suicide include talking about killing or hurting themselves, talking or writing frequently about death and dying, seeking out the means of committing suicide (e.g., guns or drugs), and significant changes in behavior. Take any talk about suicide seriously and do not try to figure out if the person really means it—get advice and help from someone who has the experience and knowledge to know what to do.

Feelings of hopelessness are also indicative of suicidal risk, such as talking about having no future, nothing to look forward to, and no possibility of things ever getting better. Other warning signs include dramatic mood or behavior changes, loss of interest in normally enjoyable activities, neglecting their appearance or self-care, and changes in eating and/or sleeping habits. Sometimes people who are contemplating suicide appear to have extremely negative self-images and seem to loathe or hate themselves. It is also common for them to get their affairs in order, saying goodbye to friends and family, giving away treasured items, withdrawing from others, and indulging in self-destructive behavior such as alcohol or drug abuse, dangerous driving, unsafe sex, reckless risk taking, and others. Finally, it is always very serious if a person who has been acutely suicidal suddenly becomes calm and even happy—this may mean that they have actually decided to kill themselves and have chosen a method. Family and friends who are concerned that someone is at risk for suicide can take some calming and subtle steps that can be helpful. Some tips are:

- Suicide Tip #1: If you are worried—say something.
  - Let the person know that you are concerned, that you care, and that you are there to help them. Tell them that you have noticed some things that are worrying you and have wondered if they would like to talk to you or someone else. You can ask them about how they are feeling and if there is something that happened recently to upset them. Often, the person will reply that no one can possibly help, and the best response is that they will not really know that until they have tried. It can also be helpful to assure them that the intense feelings at present will change, even if they do not believe it to be true.
  - When talking to a suicidal person *DO:*
    - Be yourself—do not try to be the doctor, psychologist, or the expert—be genuine and honest.
    - Listen—this is more important that what you actually say. If the person really feels that you are listening and understanding what they are saying, they are more likely to listen to you.
    - Be sympathetic, nonjudgmental, patient, calm, and accepting. It will be difficult for them to talk to you and it is a big step forward if they do.
    - Offer hope—let the person know that there really is hope, that the awful feelings they are experiencing will not last forever, and the sooner they get help the quicker they will start to feel better.

- If the person is talking about how awful they feel, do not hesitate to ask them if they feel suicidal—you will not put the idea into their head, but you can reassure them that you are willing and not afraid to talk about suicide.

  ○ When talking to a suicidal patient *DO NOT:*
    - Argue with them and try to invalidate their feelings; do not tell them how much they have to live for, or to "just look on the bright side."
    - Act shocked, lecture on the value of life, and tell them how wrong suicide is.
    - Promise confidentiality—if they are a suicidal risk you need to tell someone, but do not lie to them and tell them you will keep their "secret" and then call someone. It is OK to say something like, "I know you do not want me to tell anyone what you are planning, but I would rather have you alive and angry with me than injured or dead."
    - Offer to fix their problems or give simplistic advice. This may cause them to become more defensive and more likely to prove how hopeless their situation really is.
    - Blame yourself—their depression or emotional turmoil is not as simple as a reaction to something you may have done or said. You can apologize and then quickly tell them that, while the past cannot be changed, they can change the future by seeking assistance for this crisis.

- Suicide Tip #2—Respond quickly in a crisis.
  When you feel that someone is at risk for suicide it is important to ask questions in order to have a general understanding about the person's level of risk. You should ask questions about:

  ○ Ideation—"Are you thinking about suicide?"
  ○ Plan—"Do you have a suicide plan?"
  ○ Means—"Do you have what you need to carry out your plan?"
  ○ Time set—"Do you know when you will do it?"
  ○ Intention—"Do you expect to die by attempting suicide?"

Examples of assessing the level of risk:

- Low—some suicidal thoughts; no suicidal plan; says he/she will not commit suicide.
- Moderate—suicidal thoughts; vague plan that is not very lethal; says he/she will not commit suicide.

- High—suicidal thoughts; specific plan that is highly lethal; says he/she will not commit suicide.
- Severe—suicidal thoughts; specific plan that is highly lethal; says he/she *will* commit suicide.

Any suicide threat requires an immediate response, but the higher the risk level the more essential it is to act quickly and decisively.

- Suicide Tip #3: Offer help and support.

Being empathetic is a good place to start when trying to help someone who is at risk of suicide. Listen, let them know how much you care, and what you can do to help. You need to understand that you cannot "fix" all of their problems and you cannot "treat" them if you are not a trained professional. Remember, helping someone who is suicidal takes courage and also is very upsetting. Often it is very helpful for a person who has been dealing with someone who is suicidal to get some help and support for themselves. It may not take years of intensive therapy, but frequently a few visits with a trained professional can be very helpful for the person who is trying "to be there" for someone dealing with a suicidal crisis. If you want to be helpful to a suicidal person you have to take care of yourself first or you will not be able to help as much as you would like to. Basic steps to take to help a suicidal person to move past the moment of crisis and to seek the help they need include:

- Call for or take the person to professional help. Call 911 or the local crisis line for help or suggestions; take them to the nearest hospital emergency room; take them to their own doctor or clergy person; call a teacher, professor, resident advisor, or campus counselor.
- Follow up on their treatment—ask how treatment is going and if they are complying with the suggestions from their treating professional; call the treating professional to let them know what is going on. The treating professional cannot talk to anyone about a patient's care because of confidentiality, but they can listen or read what you tell them via the telephone, an answering machine, text, or e-mail.
- Be involved—do not just tell the person who is suicidal to "call if you need me"; be more specific. Call them, drop by, ask them to come out with you, but do not just wait to see what happens.
- Encourage positive lifestyle changes—suggest things such as healthy nutrition, getting enough sleep and exercise, being prompt with doctor appointments, taking prescribed medications, getting out of the house, and avoiding drinking alcohol or using recreational drugs.

- Make a safety plan—help the person come up with a plan that they will use if they are in crisis and feeling desperate. It means the person commits to calling their doctor or therapist, you or other friends or family; it means that they know what they are going to do at an acute crisis point.
- Remove potential means of suicide—guns, knives, razor blades, drugs should be removed from the person who is at risk with the assurance that anything legitimate that is taken away will be returned when it is safe to do so.
- Continue supporting the person beyond the crisis—often when a person is in crisis, concern and involvement from others seems plentiful, but as the situation improves, everyone seems to disappear, leaving the person with questions as to whether or not these people truly cared; stay in touch and involved.

ROLES OF PROFESSIONALS

Regardless of the feelings, beliefs, and biases of professional persons, their first and most important obligation is to their patient or the people they are serving. One of the fundamental obligations in medicine is the phrase, "First, do no harm." By agreeing to do no harm, some professionals cannot justify giving a patient a deadly drug or providing advice on how to best commit suicide. Others argue that helping someone to avoid unnecessary suffering at the end of their life is not harming a patient but is helping them. In dealing with a person who is potentially suicidal, the professional must first clarify in his or her mind that they need to focus on what is in the best interest of the patient and not on what is in their own selfish best interest.

The licensed medical or mental health professional must be strictly confidential when dealing with any patient, including a suicidal patient. The provider may not discuss any aspect of a patient's care (or even acknowledging treating the person) without the patient's expressed and written permission. Occasionally, confidentiality must be waived if a patient is an acute risk of committing suicide. However, this is not as clear to professionals as it may sound. Suppose a provider believes that a person is suicidal and calls a family member or a crisis team who then takes the patient to the hospital. Upon evaluation the patient is deemed not to be a suicidal risk. It would be within the patient's rights to charge the provider with violating their confidentiality without good cause and could even sue for damages. On the other hand, if a provider feels that a patient is a suicidal risk, but is not willing to risk violating confidentiality, and then the patient does commit suicide, the provider could be charged with negligence and malpractice and could be sued as well. In assessing the risks, the provider must avoid "overreacting" and "underreacting" since in both cases there is a risk to doing harm to the patient and putting the provider in professional and legal jeopardy. Negligence can also refer to a professional not providing good and competent treatment; if this leads to suicide the provider is professionally and legally vulnerable. Steps that providers can take to protect their patients and themselves when dealing with patients who are potentially suicidal include:

1. Discuss the patient's rights with them including the right to confidentiality, and explain the conditions under which confidentiality can be waived.
2. Explain the recommended treatment, the realistic expectations for treatment, the right to accept or reject treatment, and the meaning of "informed consent," which means that they have the right to know about the treatment being offered and must consent to it.
3. Be trained and competent to deal with suicidality, or refer the patient to someone with the training and expertise to deal with the patient's needs.
4. Be aware of the suicide risk factors and assess these periodically during treatment.
5. Be able and willing to consult with other colleagues about a case that is difficult and high risk.
6. Document the general assessment, discussion, specific types of evaluation, and treatment of suicidality. If a provider is later legally charged with something related to a suicide, their detailed documentations will be their best defense. In general, when practitioners can demonstrate prudent and responsible care in the assessment and treatment of a suicidal patient, the courts tend to favor the practitioner in legal situations.

When dealing with minor clients in cases involving suicide, legal and ethical issues may vary from one legal jurisdiction to another. For example, confidentiality issues are different when dealing with the treatment of children and adolescents. The professional will make it clear to parents and to their young clients that the client's confidentiality will always be respected unless there are issues of harm or risk. The provider is then obligated to inform the parents or others who are responsible for the safety of the child. There may be other legal considerations (e.g., abuse) when children will be treated differently from adults in similar situations. Providers must be aware of and be compliant with these issues legally, ethically, and professionally.

Family and friends can be supportive of someone who feels suicidal, but they also need to involve appropriate professionals. (Lisa F. Young/Dreamstime.com)

When a provider is evaluating a new patient for suicidal risk, it is important that the professional ask about any previous history of mental health problems or substance abuse. If there is a relevant history, then the provider will ask about previous suicide attempts or other issues of suicidality. Surprising to many, most patients will be frank about their history if they feel that the professional is nonjudgmental and is truly trying to help. Next, it is important to assess current drug or alcohol use and/or abuse. Finally, a Mental-Status Exam should be done to evaluate the patient's mood, judgment, cognitive functioning, and emotional state.

If a patient presents with any features of suicidality and/or evidence of major risk factors (e.g., major depression, bipolar disorder, schizophrenia, substance abuse, or significant stressful events in their life), it is essential that the provider ask about suicidal ideation, any plans that they may be thinking of, their intention to commit suicide, and whether or not they have access to the means and opportunity to commit suicide. The provider also needs to be aware of and assess any complications in the patient's life that might make them more vulnerable to suicidality; issues such as previous suicide attempts and even suicidal attempts by family or close friends.

The patient's presenting symptoms are also relevant, particularly feelings of helplessness and hopelessness, and anhedonia (lack of pleasure in usually rewarding activities). It is also advisable, within the constraints of confidentiality, to interview relevant family, friends, and significant others who may be able to provide information and insights that might prove helpful in developing a treatment plan. Of course, one cannot conduct these interviews without the approval and agreement of the patient, but often the client is happy to involve those who want to help them.

Questions that a provider may ask a patient who is at risk for suicide include:

1. When did you start thinking about suicide?
2. Was there anything in particular that caused you to begin thinking about suicide?
3. How often do you think about suicide?
4. Are suicidal thoughts becoming a burden to you?
5. Do you feel that your life is no longer worth living?
6. What kinds of things make you feel worse?
7. What kinds of things make you feel better?
8. Do you have a plan as to how you will kill yourself? What is your plan?

As sensitive and personal questions such as these are often reassuring to a patient that someone cares enough to ask and is not afraid of the answers. A patient can also develop the confidence that there might be someone who can help them.

Providers who are uncomfortable and harbor the same fears, misconceptions, and biases about suicide as the general public, will be ineffective in providing the special care required in these situations. The answer is improved education, opportunities to learn, and adequate supervision when dealing with at-risk patients. Providers who want to specialize in suicidal care must collaborate with and observe more senior providers and regularly participate in continuing education programs to insure that they are receiving the latest information and training. The best providers are those who continue to grow, seek new knowledge and information, look for new opportunities to improve, and who seek feedback to help improve their approach and techniques.

Dealing directly and honestly with patients is essential for a provider in any situation to be able to develop a mutually trustworthy, professional relationship. The treating provider must never mislead or try to "trick" patients because when they figure out what you have done, they will never trust you again. I also always let patients know that I assume that they are trustworthy unless they prove otherwise. For example, I have often told patients who are struggling with suicide that they need to realize that I will always believe them. If they lie, I cannot help them, but I will not play games and try to figure out "what they really mean." In order to help them, they must trust and believe that I will always be honest and open with them, and that I expect the same from them. If a patient lies or misleads the provider, it must be dealt with immediately so that treatment of the patient is not compromised.

Providers will sometimes be troubled by their own fears and misconceptions that will get in the way of adequate treatment. They may feel that the patient is "crazy" and beyond help, but they may also be frightened that they will not be able to manage the patient and may say the wrong thing, thus propelling the patient into committing suicide. Fears of the fragility of the patient and the provider's inadequacies may almost incapacitate the provider, making them far less than effective in dealing with the situation. This is the type of situation where further education, training, and supervision can be vitally helpful.

LEGAL ISSUES IN SUICIDE

As was discussed earlier, legal and societal issues related to suicide are complex and confusing. Few legal situations can force a person into treatment or hospitalization unless they are a risk to themselves or others. In the past, the United States and other countries could confine someone in prison or in hospital if they were deemed "insane." Insanity is not a medical or psychological term, but is a legal label that indicates that, due to mental and emotional problems, a person is not responsible for their own behavior. When a person is legally insane they cannot be convicted of certain crimes because they are not considered legally responsible for their own behavior. If determined to be legally insane, a judge can commit a person to an institution for care and treatment and require that necessary medication be administered. Although most judges are reluctant to take away a person's freedom, the one area where judges are likely to consider commitment and mandated treatment is when the patient is proven to be a risk to themselves and/or other people. However, in current society, patients who are hospitalized for treatment are not usually kept long enough in the facility due to insurance companies refusing to pay for intensive in-patient treatment; the companies insist that the less expensive outpatient treatment is just as adequate. Unfortunately, patients who are discharged prematurely will sometimes succeed at suicide, leaving family, friends, and doctors feeling angry and frustrated that the death of someone occurred needlessly when appropriate treatment was available but not utilized because of administrative or financial reasons.

I am personally aware of a case where a person was acutely suicidal and was hospitalized at the recommendation of his psychiatrist and psychologist. The hospital psychiatrist agreed that the person was suicidal and admitted them to the hospital. After two days the insurance company felt that the patient no longer was suicidal and did not meet the criteria for inpatient treatment and refused to pay for further hospitalization. The hospital psychiatrist and the patient's own psychologist, psychiatrist, parents, and spouse all felt that the patient was still very much at risk for suicide but because payment was removed the patient was discharged and shot himself in the head the next day. Interestingly, the hospital, hospital psychiatrist, and the patient's own psychologist and psychiatrist could be sued, but the insurance company responsible for withdrawing the care could not, by law, be sued. In this type of reimbursement climate it is very difficult to keep patients safe.

Although commitment is sometimes difficult to obtain, in many states hospitals are allowed to retain patients, who may be a risk to themselves or others, against their will for 72 hours to evaluate and stabilize them. If they need to keep the patient longer, the hospital administration has to go to court with evidence and convince a judge to agree to hospitalize the patient and to mandate treatment for a specified period of time or under certain conditions. Fortunately, many suicidal patients will agree to voluntary in-hospital treatment for a few days; this is often long enough to move the patient past the crisis and to arrange for continuing outpatient treatment. One of the major concerns in many communities is the lack of appropriate facilities to identify, care for, and keep high-risk patients safe. Particularly in small and rural communities, there may be few or no options to care for people who may be suicidal. Unfortunately, it is estimated that, on any given day, about 30,000 mental patients are confined in a jail in order to protect them because there is no place else safe to put them.

Another important legal issue related to mental health and suicide is "competence." People are assumed to be legally competent unless they have been examined by a qualified professional and deemed incompetent by a judge. In the court system, competence can have several different meanings. For example, "competent to stand trial" means that the person understands the nature and quality of their act and is able to participate in their own defense. If a person does not understand what they did and/or cannot participate in defending themselves at trial, they cannot be tried for a crime. This does not mean that they go free, but rather that they will be held in a treatment facility where they will be treated until they are able to return to court and be tried at a later time.

Competence also means that a person is able to make their own legally binding decisions. For example, a person who is judged incompetent cannot sign contracts, cannot vote, and cannot manage their own affairs, money, resources, others. The relevance of competence to suicidality can involve other legal issues; for example, in some societies it is illegal to attempt suicide, and if a person is deemed legally incompetent, they cannot be tried in court for attempting suicide. Another example is if a person attempts a legal suicide but is judged legally incompetent and the suicide attempt is assumed to be the result of the mental condition causing the person's incompetence; the person would not have the right to make their own decisions regarding treatment. In this case the court would appoint another person who is granted guardianship over the incompetent patient, and they would be able to make decisions on behalf of the patient, including decisions about treatment and hospitalization.

Another legal complication has to do with how the law treats people who have been involved with assisted suicide or voluntary euthanasia. There was a physician named Dr. Jack Kevorkian who became famous because of his very strong views on patient's right to die and the legitimate role of voluntary euthanasia. In addition to this he also provided advice to patients who wanted to end their lives peacefully and without suffering. After having helped a terminally ill patient commit suicide he was convicted of second-degree murder and was sentenced to 10–25 years in prison. He was paroled after seven years on the condition that he would not assist or provide advice for anyone regarding the commission of suicide for any reason. This case has been very important in trying to define patient's right to die in legal terms that would respect the patient but would also protect against abuse of the laws and misinterpretation that could be bad for patients and for society.

SUMMARY

Knowing and understanding the signs and risks for suicide helps us to be more helpful in a crisis situation. By approaching a suicidal person calmly and responsibly, without feeling totally responsible for keeping them alive, can offer a glimpse of hope to someone who feels helpless and hopeless. Guiding someone to take steps in the direction of getting help is the most critical decision one can make.

CHAPTER 9

Summary and Conclusions

This book examines the different issues surrounding suicide in a scholarly and professional manner, using language that is not too technical and confusing. The reader is encouraged to examine the issues surrounding suicide not only from their own moral and religious background but also with a mind open to new information and possibilities. This book was written with the intention of avoiding some of the other "agenda" that people often have about topics such as suicide.

SUICIDE—THE BASICS

The unbounded creativity of human beings has provided countless methods for suicide; it would be impossible to anticipate and prevent them all. People can use direct and active ways to commit suicide by jumping off a building, shooting themselves, or taking a bottle of pills, or they can use passive means such as not taking care of a serious medical need or continuing an unhealthy habit with the intention of dying. They can also involve other people to assist them intentionally, such as voluntary euthanasia, or less intentionally, such as "suicide by cop." The methods people may use to commit suicide will differ depending on gender, age, cultural background, religious beliefs, as well as family background, and can be intentional and voluntary.

Determining if a death was suicide, an accident, or a murder can be complex as many books, movies, and TV shows have demonstrated in their plots and counterplots, but it is the intention of the victim, which is not always clear, that can result in ruling a death a suicide or not. A "psychological autopsy" is vital for separating fact from fiction indicating a suicide, an accident, or a murder. The autopsy will consider the findings by reviewing all of the numerous possibilities of voluntary or coerced notes left behind, circumstances surrounding an accident or a staged scene, or an accidental overdose.

HISTORICAL, CULTURAL, AND RELIGIOUS PERSPECTIVE

Suicide is found in almost all societies and cultures. Some condemn it as a mortal sin, and others view it as an honorable way to die. Shortening one's own life had a different meaning in the distant past than it does in the present. Prior to the availability of antibiotics, most people died from infectious disease, even due to minor injuries, so the life expectancy was much shorter than today and the expected comfort level of people's life was usually much lower as well. Changes in medical technology and the availability of new and dramatic treatments can help keep people alive in life-threatening situations, forcing societies to readdress the meaning of voluntary or assisted suicide. Several controversial cases in recent years, exhibit patients who were apparently "brain dead" being kept alive by machines that replaced the patient's vital functions. If a patient had a "Living Will" stating that they did not want to be kept alive with machines, would this refusal to accept treatment constitute suicide? Or, if a "Health Care Proxy," someone designated by the patient to make medical decisions for them once they were unable to do so, stated that is in the patient's best interests to remove life-sustaining medical procedures, would this be "assisted suicide" or perhaps even murder? These types of medical decisions have become more and more complex, necessitating the development of fields of study such as Medical Ethics. As technology, values, and treatment possibilities change, life-sustaining methods and suicide will continue to be under scrutiny. Although most religions do not sanction suicide, many religious groups have adapted to societal and cultural changes without necessarily changing their values and beliefs. New medical guidelines such as a DNR (Do Not Resuscitate) order, the rights to deny treatment, and the use of Health Care Proxies have forced religions to reconsider their positions in light of new technologies and medical standards and practices in order to remain relevant to younger members. There will never be one belief system that suits everyone, but the differences between us forces society to think about, discuss, and find solutions for the difficult and sensitive issue of suicide.

MOTIVES AND RISK FACTORS

Although these two terms are similar, they refer to two different aspects of suicide. Motivation implies the "why" of behavior. While all behaviors are the result of some "cause," it is sometimes difficult to establish the "why" when dealing with complex behavior like suicide. An infinite number of motives or reasons can lead someone to attempt suicide, but the only thing that we know about motives is what is inferred by observing a victim's behavior. Motivation is one of the psychological factors that we can never see or measure directly, but can attempt to determine by examining behavior. Even if a person reveals what they think their motive(s) were, questions will remain about their honesty or their understanding and awareness of relevant factors leading up to the suicide attempt. Knowing the motives behind an attempt can help identify specific factors in a victim's behavior and can possibly lead to prevention, although it is important to remember that motives are fluid and may change from day to day or even hour to hour.

Risk factors may seem similar to motives and at times may be related to them, but they are quite different. They can cause a person to be more or less likely to attempt or commit suicide. Serious mental illnesses and medical problems, alcohol and drug abuse, as well as other types of behaviors, problems, and conditions, discussed previously in chapter 4, can also affect the likelihood of an attempt. The more risk factors present, the higher the risk. Motives can reveal some of the reasons why a person might want to kill themselves, and risk factors give us an idea of how likely they are to try.

PREVENTION AND TREATMENT OF SUICIDALITY

Prevention involves trying to reduce the frequency or negative impact of a particular disorder or problem—in this case, suicide. "Primary prevention" endeavors to dispense information and prevention materials to the people and places where it will have the broadest impact. "Secondary prevention" targets people in high-risk groups and tailors efforts to those with specific types of high-risk conditions (e.g., major depression, elderly divorced men, etc.). The final type of prevention, "tertiary," focuses on people who have already attempted suicide but were not successful and intends to prevent additional attempts.

Ultimately, prevention means focusing efforts and utilizing resources earlier than is typical in traditional treatment, and it requires society to decide to utilize its resources in this way. In many countries, basic fundamental needs, such as food, clothing, water, shelter, and medical care are so great that spending time and money for a possible event in the future does not rise to the level of urgency that would necessitate action. In countries with a higher standard of living, taking action to prevent suicide actually reduces the medical and human costs quite significantly, but it is often difficult to convince politicians and voters of the importance of spending money to prevent something that might not even happen. Increasing education, commitment, political activism, speaking up, and voting are some of the things that people can do to highlight the need for resources that can make a difference in prevention.

Prevention by friends and family is much more direct and can have an immediate impact. For example paying attention, listening, supporting, making suggestions are all things that someone close to a potential victim can do. In working with a potentially suicidal person, the role of the "helper" can be complicated. Friends and family members cannot take on the responsibility of treatment or watching someone twenty-four hours a day to keep them safe. The best thing to do is to behave consistently with the role that you already have with the suicidal person. Be their friend, their sibling, their parent, or whatever your relationship might be, but do not change your role when they need professional help. Call someone or take the person to a facility where help is available. If you do not know who to call, begin with calling your own doctor, a local hospital, or any adult who can help deal with a crisis.

Present treatments for suicide offer encouraging possibilities in most communities where there are well-trained professionals available. Unfortunately, people who need treatment often do not seek it either because

Keeping suicidal thoughts and feelings a secret is never a good idea—talk to someone who cares and who can help. (Monkey Business Images/Dreamstime.com)

they deny their need, they are concerned about the "stigma" of suicide, or there are no appropriate treatment options available locally. In such cases it is vital to transport the at-risk person to the nearest hospital yourself or call 911 for the police or an ambulance to assist with the situation.

CONTROVERSIAL ISSUES

The topic of suicide produces a myriad of feelings and ideas, and often very strong sentiments that usually result in controversy. In some people's minds, suicide is an extreme act by a disturbed mind—how could anyone who is sane ever want to kill themselves? Just as strongly, other people can consider suicide a rational, thoughtful, and entirely sane decision by someone facing extreme and intolerable circumstances. For most people, however, these extreme positions do not capture the complexity of figuring out exactly how they do feel about suicide. Certain types of mental illness do make some people more vulnerable to suicide, but that does not mean that all suicides are due to mental illness. On the other end of the spectrum, in some conditions a perfectly rational person might chose to end their life rather than face an impossibly difficult condition, but that does not mean that all suicides are rational. A person's attitudes and opinions are difficult to separate from culture, religious background, education and training, personal history, and personality traits of the individual who is considering suicide. The ultimate judgment on whether or not a suicide is rational or based on mental illness will depend on many issues and circumstances, but each individual's right to choose what is best for them should be respected, but this respect must be based on the awareness that the patient's decision is made with a clear mind and is a rational choice.

Few people dispute a person's "right to life," but many question the "right to death." Generally, patients have the right to be informed about their condition, to understand their treatment options, and to choose among them. Of course, this right depends on the patient's ability to make an informed choice. The controversy enters when the patient *is* competent to understand and make decisions and then chooses to die by refusing treatment or by suicide or assisted suicide. When a patient has the right to choose a treatment, it only seems reasonable that they have the right to refuse treatment as well. The ensuing debates are usually the result of issues surrounding the patient's mental capacity and their cultural or religious background. When a person chooses to end their life and enlists the assistance of someone else, it is more likely to be considered an illegal act on the part of the patient or the assisting person. This has become an important legal, social, and personal/family issue in many parts of the world, and many educated people are wrestling with this topic. It is clear that we need better legal and ethical guidelines to protect the interests of patients and their families that allow individuals to make decisions about their life as well as their death.

The relevant role of professionals, who are trained to deal with suicidal crises, is to intervene on behalf of the patient and stabilize the situation as quickly as possible. If not experienced in this area, they must refer the patient to an appropriate provider or facility. Professional roles are governed to some extent by state licensing and practice laws, but are also shaped by professional standards and the relevant standards of care for that particular profession. Too often, practitioners, and even mental health providers, deny ever dealing with suicidal patients, and research reveals that at the primary care level, PCPs (primary care physicians) typically do not inquire about history of depression, substance abuse, prior suicide attempts, or any family history of these issues. The responsibilities of professionals also include taking a complete history, acquiring records from previous providers, asking the right questions, and listening carefully to the patient, before deciding on the necessary steps to deal with the important issues that emerge. Professionals are also expected to stay current in their areas of responsibility, ask for help and supervision when needed, and to consult with other professionals when there are confusing questions or concerns. Being professional not only means doing what you can, but also recognizing situations that are beyond one's ability or training.

As discussed previously, the relevant role for family and friends who are dealing with a potentially suicidal person is simple—be yourself. It is vital that you preserve the relationship that already exists by not stepping into the role of treatment provider, even if you are professionally trained. Many people feel as though it is "up to them" to keep the person alive, and that can lead to doing things that are not helpful or that may worsen the situation.

It is essential for anyone who is trying to help a suicidal person, whether you are friend, family, concerned outsider, or treating professional, to remember several important points:

1. Regardless of your helpful intentions, you do not necessarily share the same goals with a suicidal person, and they may eventually consider you to be untrustworthy.
2. There is probably not one single thing you can say that will change their mind if they are truly suicidal.
3. You cannot, by yourself, keep them alive if they really want to die.

4. There are other people or places that can make a difference and possibly help the suicidal person.
5. There are people you (as the helper) can talk to for advice or guidance.

Hopefully, these points will prove helpful if you are ever are challenged with a possible suicide. There are no two situations exactly alike, and there are no magical words that are guaranteed to stop a suicidal person by helping them to see the error in their thinking. I do hope that this book has provided ideas and suggestions that will help people to take action as soon as they are aware someone is at risk. Knowledge is the first step and experience and wisdom will follow.

SECTION III

Primary Documents

"MAYO CLINIC: SUICIDE AND SUICIDAL THOUGHTS"

This is a comprehensive collection of information that is helpful and instructive about suicide. It is presented in a simple, easy-to-understand manner that many people will find instructive and helpful. The booklet is organized in specific sections that address the major issues in suicide. Beginning with "definitions" and "symptoms," it also focuses on "causes," "risk factors," "complications," "treatments," "prevention," and many other issues as well. It also provides contact information for suicide-prevention centers and hotlines. This site offers valuable suggestions about what they should do if someone is considering or worried about suicide, such as how to talk to a professional or how to prepare for an appointment with your doctor or mental health professional. There is also a section on what people can do to help themselves, as well as things that they should avoid to keep from making their situation even worse. Anyone who is worried about another person being suicidal, or simply wants to understand more about this issue, will find the material to be useful.

Definition

Suicide, taking your own life, is a tragic reaction to stressful life situations— and all the more tragic because suicide can be prevented. Whether you're considering suicide or know someone who feels suicidal, learn suicide warning signs and how to reach out for immediate help and professional treatment. You may save a life—your own or someone else's.

It may seem like there's no way to solve your problems and that suicide is the only way to end the pain. But you can take steps to stay safe—and start enjoying your life again.

Symptoms
Suicide warning signs or suicidal thoughts include:

- Talking about suicide—for example, making statements such as "I'm going to kill myself," "I wish I was dead" or "I wish I hadn't been born"
- Getting the means to commit suicide, such as buying a gun or stockpiling pills
- Withdrawing from social contact and wanting to be left alone
- Having mood swings, such as being emotionally high one day and deeply discouraged the next

- Being preoccupied with death, dying or violence
- Feeling trapped or hopeless about a situation
- Increasing use of alcohol or drugs
- Changing normal routine, including eating or sleeping patterns
- Doing risky or self-destructive things, such as using drugs or driving recklessly
- Giving away belongings or getting affairs in order when there is no other logical explanation for why this is being done
- Saying goodbye to people as if they won't be seen again
- Developing personality changes or being severely anxious or agitated, particularly when experiencing some of the warning signs listed above

Warning signs aren't always obvious, and they may vary from person to person. Some people make their intentions clear, while others keep suicidal thoughts and feelings secret.

When to see a doctor
If you think you may hurt yourself or attempt suicide, get help right now:

- Call 911 or your local emergency number immediately.
- Call a suicide hotline number—in the United States, call the National Suicide Prevention Lifeline at 1–800–273-TALK (1–800–273–8255) to reach a trained counselor. Use that same number and press 1 to reach the Veterans Crisis Line.

If you're feeling suicidal, but you aren't immediately thinking of hurting yourself:

- Reach out to a close friend or loved one—even though it may be hard to talk about your feelings
- Contact a minister, spiritual leader or someone in your faith community
- Call a suicide crisis center hotline
- Make an appointment with your doctor, other health care provider or mental health provider

Suicidal thinking doesn't get better on its own—so get help.

Causes
Suicidal thoughts have numerous causes. Most often, suicidal thoughts are the result of feeling like you can't cope when you're faced with what seems to be an overwhelming life situation. If you don't have hope for the future, you may mistakenly think suicide is a solution. You may experience a sort of tunnel vision, where in the middle of a crisis you believe suicide is the only way out.

There may also be a genetic link to suicide. People who complete suicide or who have suicidal thoughts or behavior are more likely to have a family history of suicide. While more research is needed to fully understand a possible genetic component, it's thought that there may be a genetic link to impulsive behavior that could contribute to suicidal tendencies.

Risk factors

Although suicide attempts are more frequent for women, men are more likely than women to complete suicide because they typically use more effective methods, such as a firearm.

You may be at risk of suicide if you:

- Feel hopeless, socially isolated or lonely
- Experience a stressful life event, such as the loss of a loved one, military service, a breakup, a significant medical illness, or financial or legal problems
- Have a substance abuse problem—alcohol and drug abuse can worsen thoughts of suicide and make you feel reckless or impulsive enough to act on your thoughts
- Have suicidal thoughts and have access to firearms in your home
- Have an underlying psychiatric disorder, such as major depression, post-traumatic stress disorder, bipolar disorder, personality disorder, anxiety or detachment from reality (psychosis), or paranoia
- Have a family history of mental disorders, substance abuse, suicide or violence, including physical or sexual abuse
- Have a medical condition that can be linked to depression and suicidal thinking, such as chronic disease, chronic pain or terminal illness
- Are bisexual, homosexual or transgender with an unsupportive family or in a hostile environment
- Attempted suicide before

Children and teenagers

Suicide in children and teenagers often follows stressful life events. Keep in mind that what a young person sees as serious and insurmountable may seem minor to an adult—such as problems in school or the loss of a friendship. In some cases, a child or teen may feel suicidal due to certain life circumstances he or she may not want to talk about. Some of these include:

- Having a psychiatric disorder, including depression
- Loss or conflict with close friends or family members
- History of physical or sexual abuse
- Problems with alcohol or drugs
- Becoming pregnant

- Having a sexually transmitted infection
- Being the victim of bullying
- Being uncertain of sexual orientation

Murder and suicide

In some cases, people, who are suicidal, are at risk of killing others and then themselves. This is known as a homicide-suicide or murder-suicide. The types of feelings that trigger this tragic behavior can stem from a number of sources. Some common risk factors for murder-suicide include:

- History of conflict with a spouse or romantic partner
- Current family legal or financial problems
- History of mental health problems, particularly depression
- Alcohol or drug abuse or addiction
- Having access to a firearm—nearly all murder-suicides are committed using a gun

Starting antidepressants and increased suicide risk

Some studies have shown a possible link between starting treatment with an antidepressant and an increased risk of suicide. The Food and Drug Administration (FDA) requires manufacturers of all antidepressants to include a warning stating that antidepressants may increase suicide risk in children, adolescents and young adults during the first few months of treatment.

However, the link between antidepressants and suicidal thinking isn't clear—and not taking an antidepressant when it's needed also increases the risk of suicide. To be safe, anyone who starts taking an antidepressant should be watched closely for signs of suicidal thinking. If you—or someone you know—has suicidal thoughts when taking an antidepressant, immediately contact your doctor or get emergency help.

Complications

Suicidal thoughts and attempted suicide take an emotional toll, both for those who want to take their own life and for their loved ones. For instance, you may be so consumed by suicidal thoughts that you can't function in your daily life. And while many suicide attempts are impulsive acts during a moment of crisis, they can leave you with permanent serious or debilitating injuries, such as organ failure or brain damage.

For those left behind after a suicide—people known as survivors of suicide—grief, anger, depression and guilt are common.

Preparing for your appointment

When you call your primary care doctor to set up an appointment, you may be referred immediately to a psychiatrist. If you're in danger of committing suicide, your doctor may have you get emergency help at the hospital.

What you can do

Take these steps before your appointment:

- *Write down key personal information,* including any major stresses or recent life changes.
- *Make a list of all medications,* vitamins and supplements that you're taking.
- *Take a family member or friend along* if possible—someone who accompanies you may remember something that you missed or forgot.
- *Write down questions* to ask your doctor.

Some basic questions to ask your doctor include:

- Are my suicidal thoughts most likely linked to an underlying mental or physical health problem?
- Other than the most likely cause, what are other possible causes?
- Will I need any tests for possible underlying conditions?
- Do I need immediate treatment of some kind? What will that involve?
- What are the alternatives to the approach that you're suggesting?
- I have these other mental or physical health problems. How can I best manage them together?
- Is there anything special I should do to stay safe and feel better?
- Should I see a psychiatrist? Will my insurance cover it?
- Is there a generic alternative to the medicine you're prescribing me?
- Are there any brochures or other printed material that I can take home with me? What websites do you recommend?

Don't hesitate to ask questions during your appointment when you don't understand something.

What to expect from your doctor

Your doctor is likely to ask you a number of questions. To save time, be ready to answer them.

- When did you first begin having suicidal thoughts?
- Have your suicidal thoughts been continuous or occasional?
- Have you ever tried to commit suicide?
- Do you have a plan to kill yourself now?
- If you have a plan, does it involve a specific method, place or time?
- Have you made any preparations, such as gathering pills, changing your will or writing suicide notes?
- Do you feel like you can control your impulses when you feel reckless or like killing or hurting yourself?
- Do you have friends or family members you can talk to or go to for help?
- What are your feelings about the future? Do you have any hope that things will improve?

- Do you drink alcohol, and if so, how much and how often?
- What medications do you take?
- Do you use illegal drugs?
- What, if anything, seems to improve your suicidal thoughts?
- What, if anything, appears to worsen your suicidal thoughts?

What you can do in the meantime

If you've scheduled an appointment and can't see your doctor immediately, make sure you stay safe. Contact family members, friends or other people you trust to help you. If you feel you're in danger of hurting yourself or attempting suicide, call 911 or get emergency help immediately.

Tests and diagnosis

Your doctor may do a physical exam, tests and in-depth questioning about your mental and physical health to help determine what may be causing your suicidal thinking and to determine the best treatment.

Mental health conditions

In most cases, suicidal thoughts are linked to an underlying mental health issue that can be treated. If this is the case, you may need to see a doctor who specializes in diagnosing and treating mental illness (psychiatrist) or other mental health provider.

Physical causes

In some cases, suicidal thinking may be linked to an underlying physical health problem. You may need blood tests and other tests to determine whether this is the case.

Alcohol and drugs

For many people, alcohol or drugs play a role in suicidal thinking and completed suicide. Your doctor will want to know whether you have any problems with alcohol or drug use—such as bingeing or being unable to cut back or quit using alcohol on your own. Many people who feel suicidal need treatment to help them stop using alcohol or drugs for their suicidal feelings to improve.

In some people, certain prescription or over-the-counter drugs can cause suicidal feelings. Tell your doctor about any medications you take to see whether they could be linked to your suicidal thinking.

Children and teenagers

Children who are feeling suicidal usually need to see a psychiatrist or psychologist experienced in diagnosing and treating children with mental health problems. The doctor will want to get an accurate picture of what's going on from a variety of sources, such as the young person, parents or guardians, other people close to the child, school reports, and previous medical or psychiatric evaluations.

Treatments and drugs

Treatment of suicidal thoughts and behavior depends on your specific situation, including your level of suicide risk and what underlying problems may be causing your suicidal thoughts or behavior.

Emergencies

If you've made a suicide attempt and you're injured:

- Call 911 or your local emergency number
- Have someone else call if you're not alone

If you're not injured, but you're at immediate risk of harming yourself:

- Call 911 or your local emergency number
- Call a suicide hotline number—in the United States, call the National Suicide Prevention Lifeline at 1–800–273-TALK (1–800–273–8255) to reach a trained counselor. Use that same number and press 1 to reach the Veterans Crisis Line.

At the emergency room, you'll be treated for any injuries. The doctor will ask you a number of questions and may examine you, looking for recent or past signs of suicide attempts. Depending on your state of mind, you may need medications to calm you or to ease symptoms of an underlying mental illness, such as depression.

Your doctor may want you to stay in the hospital long enough to make sure any treatments are working, that you'll be safe when you leave and that you'll get the follow-up treatment you need.

Nonemergency situations

If you have suicidal thoughts, but aren't in a crisis situation, you may need outpatient treatment. This treatment may include:

- **Psychotherapy.** In psychotherapy, also called counseling or talk therapy, you explore the issues that make you feel suicidal. You and your therapist can work together to develop treatment plans and goals.
- **Medications.** Antidepressants, antipsychotic medications, anti-anxiety medications and other medications for mental illness can help reduce symptoms, which can help you feel less suicidal.

- **Addiction treatment.** Treatment for drug or alcohol addiction can include detoxification, addiction treatment programs and self-help group meetings.
- **Family support and education.** Your loved ones can be both a source of support and conflict. Involving them in treatment can help them understand what you're going through, give them better coping skills, and improve family communication and relationships.

Helping a loved one with suicidal thoughts

If you have a loved one who has attempted suicide, or if you think your loved one may be in danger of doing so, get emergency help.

If you have a loved one you think may be considering suicide, have an open and honest discussion about your concerns. You may not be able to force someone to seek professional care, but you can offer encouragement and support. You can also help your loved one find a qualified doctor or mental health provider and make an appointment. You may even be able to go to an appointment with him or her.

Supporting a loved one who is chronically suicidal can be stressful and exhausting. You may be afraid and feel guilty and helpless. Take advantage of resources about suicide and suicide prevention so that you have information and tools to take action when needed. Also, be sure to take care of yourself by getting support from family, friends, organizations and professionals.

Lifestyle and home remedies

There's no substitute for professional help when it comes to treating suicidal thinking and preventing suicide. However, there are a few things that may reduce suicide risk:

- **Avoid drugs and alcohol.** Alcohol and illegal drugs can worsen suicidal thoughts. They can also make you feel less inhibited, which means you're more likely to act on your thoughts.
- **Form a strong support network.** That may include family, friends or members of your church, synagogue or other place of worship. Religious practice has been shown to help reduce the risk of suicide.
- **Get active.** Physical activity and exercise have been shown to reduce depression symptoms. Consider walking, jogging, swimming, gardening or taking up another form of physical activity that you enjoy.

Coping and support

Don't try to manage suicidal thoughts or behavior entirely on your own. You need professional help and support to overcome the problems linked to suicidal thinking. In addition:

- **Go to your appointments.** Don't skip therapy sessions or doctor's appointments, even if you don't want to go or don't feel like you need to.
- **Take medications as directed.** Even if you're feeling well, don't skip your medications. If you stop, your suicidal feelings may come back. You could

also experience withdrawal-like symptoms from abruptly stopping an anti-depressant or other medication.
- **Learn about your condition.** Learning about your condition can empower and motivate you to stick to your treatment plan. If you have depression, for instance, learn about its causes and treatments.
- **Pay attention to warning signs.** Work with your doctor or therapist to learn what might trigger your suicidal feelings. Make a plan so you know what to do if suicidal thoughts return. Contact your doctor or therapist if you notice any changes in how you feel. Consider involving family members or friends in watching for warning signs.
- **Seek help from a support group.** A number of organizations are available to help you cope with suicidal thinking and recognize that there are many options in your life other than suicide.

Prevention
To help keep yourself from feeling suicidal:

- **Get the treatment you need.** If you don't treat the underlying cause, your suicidal thoughts are likely to return. You may feel embarrassed to seek treatment for your mental health problems, but getting the right treatment for depression, substance abuse or another underlying problem will make you feel better about life—and help keep you safe.
- **Follow your treatment plan.** Go to follow-up appointments, take medications exactly as directed, and take the other steps your doctor or mental health provider recommends.
- **Know your warning signs and make a plan.** Learn to spot the danger signs early, and decide what steps to take ahead of time. It may help to write out what steps you'll take if you start feeling suicidal. You may want to make a written agreement with a mental health provider or a loved one to help you anticipate the right steps to take when you don't have the best judgment. Clearly stating your suicidal intention with your therapist makes it possible to anticipate it and address it.
- **Eliminate potential means of committing suicide.** If you think you might act on suicidal thoughts, immediately get rid of any potential means of committing suicide, such as firearms, knives or dangerous medications. If you take medications that have a potential for overdose, have a family member or friend give you your medications as prescribed.
- **Establish your support network.** It may be hard to talk about suicidal feelings, and your friends and family may not fully understand why you feel the way you do. Reach out anyway, and make sure the people who care about you know what's going on and are there when you need them. You may also want to get help from your place of worship, support groups or other community resources.
- **Remember, suicidal feelings are temporary.** If you feel hopeless or that life's not worth living anymore, remember that the feelings will pass. Take

one step at a time and don't act impulsively. Work to regain your perspective—and life will get better.

Source: Mayo Clinic. Available at: http://www.mayoclinic.com/health/suicide/DS01062. Used by permission of the Mayo Clinic.

"Suicide by Profession: Lots of Confusion, Inconclusive Data"

There are many myths about suicide in various professions, but many of the studies are questionable and often there are conflicting results and findings. White male physicians, African Americans in guard positions, such as security personnel, and women in the arts seem to be at higher risk, but even then the percentages are very small and difficult to generalize. Many published studies focus on only one geographic area, and obtaining data is challenging. For example, not all states require the cause of death on the death certificate, and there may not be an indication that it was suicide (e.g., gunshot wound).

Another issue in linking suicide to specific professions is that simply being in a particular profession says very little about the individual. For example, if it is true that white physicians are higher risk for suicide, then what are the characteristics of those physicians who do not attempt suicide and how do they differ from at-risk physicians?

It is tempting to take specific pieces of information (e.g., profession) that seem to be linked to suicide and then generalize from that single variable. Suicide is very complex and will never be explained with a simple relationship. Researchers need to consider what it is about those particular professions that lead to higher suicide rates, and also what is it about the individual suicide victims that make them different and more vulnerable than their colleagues who do not attempt suicide?

Police officers end their lives more often than those in other professions, right? Or is it dentists? Or psychologists?

Assertions about which occupational group has the most suicides float around like urban myths.

Various occupational groups have called the National Center for Health Statistics (NCHS), each to confirm that their occupation has the highest rates of suicide, says Jim Weed, NCHS analyst.

But experts on suicide say that statistics on its relation to occupation are not clear. There is no national data set on occupation and suicide. Local studies indicate elevated rates in different occupations, but the data usually "turn out to be frail," says prominent suicide researcher David Clark, PhD.

And in fact, points out Ronald Maris, PhD, director of the Center for the Study of Suicide and Life-Threatening Behavior at the University of South Carolina, "Occupation is not a major predictor of suicide and it does not explain much about why the person commits suicide."

One of the largest studies in the area was conducted by the National Institute of Occupational Safety and Health (NIOSH) in 1995, which concluded that there is a higher suicide rate in the medical field. But beyond that, NIOSH researchers said, the picture is equivocal: Often the studies are only of one geographic area, sometimes they have methodological problems, and sometimes they contradict each other.

That's in great part because the statistics are surprisingly difficult to gather. Only about half the states put occupation on their death certificates. And even when they do, there are questions as to whether the physician, medical examiner or coroner filling in the certificates always gets the occupation or the cause of death right.

In addition, statistical conclusions are hampered by the fact that when the 30,000 annual U.S. suicides are divided into occupations, the numbers for many job categories are relatively small.

Some larger studies in the last few years provide at least some thought-provoking questions about connections between jobs and suicide. For example, in 1997, NIOSH and other government agencies analyzed 1980–84 death certificates by all occupations and causes of death, and found statistically significant elevated rates of suicide for:

- White male physicians.
- Black male guards (including supervisors, crossing guards, police, protective service occupations, but not correctional institution occupations).
- White female painters, sculptors, craft-artists and artist printmakers.

Source: K. Foxhall, "Suicide by Profession: Lots of Confusion, Inconclusive Data." *Monitor on Psychology,* January 2001, Vol. 32, No. 1. Print version: page 19. Available at: http://www.apa.org/monitor/jan01/suicide.aspx. American Psychological Association. Adapted with permission.

"EXPLORING THE LINK BETWEEN SUICIDE AND TBI"

This article discusses the link between traumatic brain injury (TBI) and suicide, and much of their data comes from studies on American military personnel who have developed TBI due to injuries during combat. One disturbing statistic reveals that, in recent years, more soldiers died from suicide than from combat injuries, and since many of the victims were suffering from TBI, this relationship has become the focus of concern and further evaluation.

Studies from other countries have also demonstrated the relationship between TBI and suicide, and they have discovered that many people with TBI also struggle with feelings of hopelessness. It is well established in the research literature that feelings of helplessness and hopelessness are common in patients suffering from depression, and feelings of hopelessness are often core to the experience of people who are high risk for suicide. It is not surprising that people suffering from TBI frequently experience a sense of loss due to their injuries and coupled with

feelings of helplessness and hopelessness, are more susceptible to depression and
suicidality.

If people who are potentially suicidal can be identified and treated earlier,
there is a greater chance of a positive result. Of course, most people with TBI are
neither depressed nor suicidal, but it seems clear that when dealing with patients
who have TBI, attention should be given to their mental state, the possibility of
depression, and the heightened risk of suicide.

Earlier this year, the Pentagon reported an extremely grim statistic: In the first
months of the year, a soldier was more likely to die from suicide than from war
injuries. From early January to early May 2012, the suicide rate averaged nearly
one per day among active-duty troops—an 18 percent increase from last year. Suicide rates among veterans are equally daunting. According to an estimate from the
Department of Veterans Affairs (VA), a veteran dies by suicide every 80 minutes.

In August, President Barack Obama signed an executive order that strength-
ened suicide prevention efforts for service members and veterans. Among the
many efforts being funded and watched by the Department of Defense (DoD) are
those of Lisa Brenner, PhD, who is working with colleagues to adapt a civilian
suicide prevention intervention for military personnel and veterans with traumatic
brain injury (TBI).

Brenner directs the VA's Mental Illness Research, Education and Clinical Center (MIRECC) in Denver and Salt Lake City, one of 10 such VA centers designed to
be incubators of innovative research and treatment. Each center has a specific mission; in Denver, Brenner and her colleagues study ways to prevent suicide among
veterans. They have about 30 ongoing research projects. Funding is from the VA,
DoD, and non-federal sources including the State of Colorado TBI Trust Fund.

One project explored whether a history of TBI increases suicide risk among
veterans and service personnel. "We're just beginning to figure that out," she says.

Brenner led a study examining suicide risk in 49,626 VA patients with a history of TBI. The team's findings show that, overall, veterans with TBI have an
increased risk of dying by suicide compared with veterans without brain injuries. This is consistent with findings among members of the general population.
The analysis was published in the July/August 2011 issue of the *Journal of Head
Trauma Rehabilitation.*

Evidence-based interventions for those with TBI are needed, Brenner adds.
That's where her work with Grahame Simpson, PhD, of the Liverpool Hospital/
Ingham Institute of Applied Medical Research in Sydney, Australia, comes in. He
developed the Window to Hope program, which focuses on relieving feelings of
hopelessness among patients with TBI. Previous research has shown that hopelessness is a stronger predictor of eventual suicide than depression.

Source: Rebecca Voelker, "Exploring the Link between Suicide and TBI." *Monitor on
Psychology.* December 2012, Vol. 43, No. 11. Print version: page 38. Available at: http://
www.apa.org/monitor/2012/12/suicide-tbi.aspx American Psychological Association.
Adapted with permission.

"SUICIDES"

This is a very powerful story by Guy de Maupassant that is short and easy to read, but is particularly effective in showing the depth of desperation, loneliness, and resignation that seems to accompany the suicides of many people. The reader can feel that the suicide victim in this story truly cannot conceive of a life without the pain and misery that he has experienced for the previous 30 years. While most of us may have difficulty imagining feeling like that for more than a short time, many suicide victims appear to share these types of thoughts and feelings. This story also brings to life the feelings of helplessness and hopelessness that often trouble people who are at risk for suicide. The fact that this short piece is written by a brilliant author, who is known as one of the greatest short story authors, makes the work even more powerful because of his artful use of language and images.

Tragically, de Maupassant was all too familiar with pain, misery, and mental anguish. In fact he did attempt to kill himself later in life and was then committed to a hospital for the treatment of mental illness. He had become very unhappy and unable to experience any pleasure in a life filled with suspicion and misery. His depression and psychological disturbance was probably caused in part or wholly by the syphilis that he had contracted as a youth, which finally spread to his brain.

To Georges Legrand.

Hardly a day goes by without our reading a news item like the following in some newspaper:

"On Wednesday night the people living in No. 40 Rue de——, were awakened by two successive shots. The explosions seemed to come from the apartment occupied by M. X——. The door was broken in and the man was found bathed in his blood, still holding in one hand the revolver with which he had taken his life.

"M. X——was fifty-seven years of age, enjoying a comfortable income, and had everything necessary to make him happy. No cause can be found for his action."

What terrible grief, what unknown suffering, hidden despair, secret wounds drive these presumably happy persons to suicide? We search, we imagine tragedies of love, we suspect financial troubles, and, as we never find anything definite, we apply to these deaths the word "mystery."

A letter found on the desk of one of these "suicides without cause," and written during his last night, beside his loaded revolver, has come into our hands. We deem it rather interesting. It reveals none of those great catastrophes which we always expect to find behind these acts of despair; but it shows us the slow succession of the little vexations of life, the disintegration of a lonely existence, whose dreams have disappeared; it gives the reason for these tragic ends, which only nervous and high-strung people can understand.

Here it is:

"It is midnight. When I have finished this letter I shall kill myself. Why? I shall attempt to give the reasons, not for those who may read these lines, but for myself, to kindle my waning courage, to impress upon myself the fatal necessity of this act which can, at best, be only deferred.

"I was brought up by simple-minded parents who were unquestioning believers. And I believed as they did.

"My dream lasted a long time. The last veil has just been torn from my eyes.

"During the last few years a strange change has been taking place within me. All the events of Life, which formerly had to me the glow of a beautiful sunset, are now fading away. The true meaning of things has appeared to me in its brutal reality; and the true reason for love has bred in me disgust even for this poetic sentiment: 'We are the eternal toys of foolish and charming illusions, which are always being renewed'.

"On growing older, I had become partly reconciled to the awful mystery of life, to the uselessness of effort; when the emptiness of everything appeared to me in a new light, this evening, after dinner.

"Formerly, I was happy! Everything pleased me: the passing women, the appearance of the streets, the place where I lived; and I even took an interest in the cut of my clothes. But the repetition of the same sights has had the result of filling my heart with weariness and disgust, just as one would feel were one to go every night to the same theatre.

"For the last thirty years I have been rising at the same hour; and, at the same restaurant, for thirty years, I have been eating at the same hours the same dishes brought me by different waiters.

"I have tried travel. The loneliness which one feels in strange places terrified me. I felt so alone, so small on the earth that I quickly started on my homeward journey.

"But here the unchanging expression of my furniture, which has stood for thirty years in the same place, the smell of my apartments (for, with time, each dwelling takes on a particular odor) each night, these and other things disgust me and make me sick of living thus.

"Everything repeats itself endlessly. The way in which I put my key in the lock, the place where I always find my matches, the first object which meets my eye when I enter the room, make me feel like jumping out of the window and putting an end to those monotonous events from which we can never escape.

"Each day, when I shave, I feel an inordinate desire to cut my throat; and my face, which I see in the little mirror, always the same, with soap on my cheeks, has several times made me weak from sadness.

"Now I even hate to be with people whom I used to meet with pleasure; I know them so well, I can tell just what they are going to say and what I am going to answer. Each brain is like a circus, where the same horse keeps circling around eternally. We must circle round always, around the same ideas, the same joys, the same pleasures, the same habits, the same beliefs, the same sensations of disgust.

"The fog was terrible this evening. It enfolded the boulevard, where the street lights were dimmed and looked like smoking candles. A heavier weight than usual oppressed me. Perhaps my digestion was bad.

"For good digestion is everything in life. It gives the inspiration to the artist, amorous desires to young people, clear ideas to thinkers, the joy of life to everybody, and it also allows one to eat heartily (which is one of the greatest pleasures). A sick stomach induces skepticism unbelief, nightmares and the desire for death. I have often noticed this fact. Perhaps I would not kill myself, if my digestion had been good this evening.

"When I sat down in the arm-chair where I have been sitting every day for thirty years, I glanced around me, and just then I was seized by such a terrible distress that I thought I must go mad.

"I tried to think of what I could do to run away from myself. Every occupation struck me as being worse even than inaction. Then I bethought me of putting my papers in order.

"For a long time I have been thinking of clearing out my drawers; for, for the last thirty years, I have been throwing my letters and bills pell-mell into the same desk, and this confusion has often caused me considerable trouble. But I feel such moral and physical laziness at the sole idea of putting anything in order that I have never had the courage to begin this tedious business.

"I therefore opened my desk, intending to choose among my old papers and destroy the majority of them.

"At first I was bewildered by this array of documents, yellowed by age, then I chose one.

"Oh! if you cherish life, never disturb the burial place of old letters!

"And if, perchance, you should, take the contents by the handful, close your eyes that you may not read a word, so that you may not recognize some forgotten handwriting which may plunge you suddenly into a sea of memories; carry these papers to the fire; and when they are in ashes, crush them to an invisible powder, or otherwise you are lost—just as I have been lost for an hour.

"The first letters which I read did not interest me greatly. They were recent, and came from living men whom I still meet quite often, and whose presence does not move me to any great extent. But all at once one envelope made me start. My name was traced on it in a large, bold handwriting; and suddenly tears came to my eyes. That letter was from my dearest friend, the companion of my youth, the confidant of my hopes; and he appeared before me so clearly, with his pleasant smile and his hand outstretched, that a cold shiver ran down my back. Yes, yes, the dead come back, for I saw him! Our memory is a more perfect world than the universe: it gives back life to those who no longer exist.

"With trembling hand and dimmed eyes I reread everything that he told me, and in my poor sobbing heart I felt a wound so painful that I began to groan as a man whose bones are slowly being crushed.

"Then I travelled over my whole life, just as one travels along a river. I recognized people, so long forgotten that I no longer knew their names. Their faces alone lived in me. In my mother's letters I saw again the old servants, the shape of our house and the little insignificant odds and ends which cling to our minds.

"Yes, I suddenly saw again all my mother's old gowns, the different styles which she adopted and the several ways in which she dressed her hair. She haunted me especially in a silk dress, trimmed with old lace; and I remembered something she said one day when she was wearing this dress. She said: 'Robert, my child, if you do not stand up straight you will be round-shouldered all your life'.

"Then, opening another drawer, I found myself face to face with memories of tender passions: a dancing-pump, a torn handkerchief, even a garter, locks of hair and dried flowers. Then the sweet romances of my life, whose living heroines are now white-haired, plunged me into the deep melancholy of things. Oh, the young brows where blond locks curl, the caress of the hands, the glance which speaks, the hearts which beat, that smile which promises the lips, those lips which promise the embrace! And the first kiss-that endless kiss which makes you close your eyes, which drowns all thought in the immeasurable joy of approaching possession!

"Taking these old pledges of former love in both my hands, I covered them with furious caresses, and in my soul, torn by these memories, I saw them each again at the hour of surrender; and I suffered a torture more cruel than all the tortures invented in all the fables about hell.

"One last letter remained. It was written by me and dictated fifty years ago by my writing teacher. Here it is:

"'MY DEAR LITTLE MAMMA:

"'I am seven years old to-day. It is the age of reason. I take advantage of it to thank you for having brought me into this world.

"'Your little son, who loves you

"'ROBERT'.

"It is all over. I had gone back to the beginning, and suddenly I turned my glance on what remained to me of life. I saw hideous and lonely old age, and approaching infirmities, and everything over and gone. And nobody near me!

"My revolver is here, on the table. I am loading it. . . . Never reread your old letters!"

And that is how many men come to kill themselves; and we search in vain to discover some great sorrow in their lives.

Source: Guy de Maupassant, "Suicides." From "Original Short Stories, translated by Albert M.C. McMaster, A.E. Henderson, MME. Quesada, and others. Originally published on August 29, 1880, in the French newspaper Le Gaulois.

UCR Today—"Study Links Suicide Risk with Rates of Gun Ownership, Political Conservatism"

This particular research and the accompanying story is a good example of how political and religious issues may be related to suicide, and for the nonstatistician the differences between a causal relationship and a correlation are frequently misunderstood. This study concludes that there is a statistical relationship between gun ownership, political conservatism, church membership, and the incidence of suicide. It is tempting to conclude that these factors cause suicide, but it is not that simple. According to statisticians the four variables mentioned above are correlated but would assert that "correlation does not imply causation." They might have a causal link, they might involve additional factors that can affect all of the above variables, or there might not be a causal relationship at all—there is simply no way to tell from reviewing this data alone.

However, these variables are clearly related in some manner, and this cannot be ignored either. Since political, social, and religious issues often are central to discussions about suicide, keeping an open mind and looking at the data objectively and honestly is important when trying to make sense of complex phenomena such as suicide. We may not find the answers that we want, but we have to be open to the possibility that further information may lead to levels of understanding that might actually help us understand suicide better.

UCR study links risk of suicide with rate of gun ownership and political conservatism at the state level.

RIVERSIDE, Calif.—Residents of states with the highest rates of gun ownership and political conservatism are at greater risk of suicide than those in states with less gun ownership and less politically conservative leanings, according to a study by University of California, Riverside sociology professor Augustine J. Kposowa.

The study, "Association of suicide rates, gun ownership, conservatism and individual suicide risk," was published online in the journal *Social Psychiatry & Psychiatric Epidemiology* in February.

Suicide was the 11th leading cause of death for all ages in the United States in 2007, the most recent year for which complete mortality data was available at the time of the study. It was the seventh leading cause of death for males and the 15th leading cause of death for females. Firearms are the most commonly used method of suicide by males and poisoning the most common among females.

Kposowa, who has studied suicide and its causes for two decades, analyzed mortality data from the U.S. Multiple Cause of Death Files for 2000 through 2004 and combined individual-level data with state-level information. Firearm ownership, conservatism (measured by percentage voting for former President George W. Bush in the 2000 election), suicide rate, church adherence, and the immigration rate were measured at the state level. He analyzed data relating to 131,636 individual suicides, which were then compared to deaths from natural causes (excluding homicides and accidents).

"Many studies show that of all suicide methods, firearms have the highest case fatality, implying that an individual who selects this technique has a very low chance of survival," Kposowa said. Guns are simply the most efficient method of suicide, he added.

With few exceptions, states with the highest rates of gun ownership—for example, Alaska, Montana, Wyoming, Idaho, Alabama, and West Virginia—also tended to have the highest suicide rates. These states were also carried overwhelmingly by George Bush in the 2000 presidential election.

The study also found that:

- The odds of committing suicide were 2.9 times higher among men than women
- Non-Hispanic whites were nearly four times as likely to kill themselves as Non-Hispanic African Americans
- The odds of suicide among Hispanics were 2.3 times higher than the odds among Non-Hispanic African Americans
- Divorced and separated individuals were 38 percent more likely to kill themselves than those who were married
- A higher percentage of church-goers at the state level reduced individual suicide risk.

"Church adherence may promote church attendance, which exposes an individual to religious beliefs, for example, about an afterlife. Suicide is proscribed in the three monotheistic religions: Judaism, Christianity and Islam," Kposowa noted in explaining the finding that church membership at the state level reduces individual risk of suicide. "In states with a higher percentage of the population that belong to a church, it is plausible that religious views and doctrine about suicide are well-known through sacred texts, theology or sermons, and adherents may be less likely to commit suicide."

Kposowa is the first to use a nationally representative sample to examine the effect of firearm availability on suicide odds. Previous studies that associated firearm availability to suicide were limited to one or two counties. His study also demonstrates that individual behavior is influenced not only by personal characteristics, but by social structural or contextual attributes. That is, what happens at the state level can influence the personal actions of those living within that state.

The sociologist said that although policies aimed at seriously regulating firearm ownership would reduce individual suicides, such policies are likely to fail not because they do not work, but because many Americans remain opposed to meaningful gun control, arguing that they have a constitutional right to bear arms.

"Even modest efforts to reform gun laws are typically met with vehement opposition. There are also millions of Americans who continue to believe that keeping a gun at home protects them against intruders, even though research shows that when a gun is used in the home, it is often against household members in the commission of homicides or suicides," Kposowa said.

"Adding to the widespread misinformation about guns is that powerful pro-gun lobby groups, especially the National Rifle Association, seem to have a stranglehold on legislators and U.S. policy, and a politician who calls for gun control may be targeted for removal from office in a future election by a gun lobby," he added.

Although total suicide rates in the U.S. are not much higher than in other Western countries, without changes in gun-ownership policies "the United States is poised to remain a very armed and potentially dangerous nation for its inhabitants for years to come."

Source: Bettye Miller, "Suicide Risk Linked to Gun Ownership and Political Conservatism." *UCR Today,* April 4, 2013. Available at: http://ucrtoday.ucr.edu/13287. Used by permission of University of California, Riverside.

"ABOUT TEEN SUICIDE"

This is a brief and informative pamphlet-type of site that provides a wealth of information about suicide, specifically in teens. It is directed toward parents, but is appropriate for teens to read as well. Although many specific facts are shared, it is not just a list of research findings. This site provides suggestions and ideas that are useful when dealing with a person who is high risk for suicide, or even if they are feeling suicidal themselves. Factual information is presented accurately without seeming dull or boring; it also explores ideas with a sense of importance and emotion but without sounding alarming or exaggerating the risks.

There is nothing as tragic as a parent losing a child, especially as a result of suicide. Parents will frequently comment that it does not seem real and that they still cannot believe it. This short article offers suggestions to survivors of a suicidal death that can be helpful in reducing or reversing the feeling of being totally powerless.

This site and/or the pamphlet would be very appropriate to have available in the counseling office at schools, in libraries, and in doctors', psychologists', and social workers' offices. It answers many questions and provides some helpful and direct advice without being overly dramatic.

The tragedy of a young person dying because of overwhelming hopelessness or frustration is devastating to family, friends, and community. Parents, siblings, classmates, coaches, and neighbors might be left wondering if they could have done something to prevent that young person from turning to suicide.

Learning more about factors that might lead an adolescent to suicide may help prevent further tragedies. Even though it's not always preventable, it's always a good idea to be informed and take action to help a troubled teenager.

About Teen Suicide

The reasons behind a teen's suicide or attempted suicide can be complex. Although suicide is relatively rare among children, the rate of suicides and suicide attempts increases tremendously during adolescence.

Suicide is the third-leading cause of death for 15- to 24-year-olds, according to the Centers for Disease Control and Prevention (CDC), after accidents and homicide. It's also thought that at least 25 attempts are made for every completed teen suicide.

The risk of suicide increases dramatically when kids and teens have access to firearms at home, and nearly 60% of all suicides in the United States are committed with a gun. That's why any gun in your home should be unloaded, locked, and kept out of the reach of children and teens.

Overdose using over-the-counter, prescription, and non-prescription medicine is also a very common method for both attempting and completing suicide. It's important to monitor carefully all medications in your home. Also be aware that teens will "trade" different prescription medications at school and carry them (or store them) in their locker or backpack.

Suicide rates differ between boys and girls. Girls think about and attempt suicide about twice as often as boys, and tend to attempt suicide by overdosing on drugs or cutting themselves. Yet boys die by suicide about four times as often girls, perhaps because they tend to use more lethal methods, such as firearms, hanging, or jumping from heights.

Which Teens Are at Risk for Suicide?

It can be hard to remember how it felt to be a teen, caught in that gray area between childhood and adulthood. Sure, it's a time of tremendous possibility but it also can be a period of stress and worry. There's pressure to fit in socially, to perform academically, and to act responsibly.

Adolescence is also a time of sexual identity and relationships and a need for independence that often conflicts with the rules and expectations set by others.

Young people with mental health problems—such as anxiety, depression, bipolar disorder, or insomnia—are at higher risk for suicidal thoughts. Teens going through major life changes (parents' divorce, moving, a parent leaving home due to military service or parental separation, financial changes) and those who are victims of bullying are at greater risk of suicidal thoughts.

Factors that increase the risk of suicide among teens include:

- a psychological disorder, especially <u>depression</u>, bipolar disorder, and <u>alcohol</u> and <u>drug use </u>(in fact, approximately 95% of people who die by suicide have a psychological disorder at the time of death)
- feelings of distress, irritability, or agitation
- feelings of hopelessness and worthlessness that often accompany depression
- a previous suicide attempt
- a family history of depression or suicide
- emotional, physical, or sexual abuse
- lack of a support network, poor relationships with parents or peers, and feelings of social isolation
- dealing with bisexuality or homosexuality in an unsupportive family or community or hostile school environment

Warning Signs

Suicide among teens often occurs following a stressful life event, such as problems at school, a breakup with a boyfriend or girlfriend, the death of a loved one, a divorce, or a major family conflict.

Teens who are thinking about suicide might:

- talk about suicide or death in general
- give hints that they might not be around anymore
- talk about feeling hopeless or feeling guilty
- pull away from friends or family
- write songs, poems, or letters about death, separation, and loss
- start giving away treasured possessions to siblings or friends
- lose the desire to take part in favorite things or activities
- have trouble concentrating or thinking clearly
- experience changes in eating or sleeping habits
- engage in risk-taking behaviors
- lose interest in school or sports

What Can Parents Do?

Many teens who commit or attempt suicide have given some type of warning to loved ones ahead of time. So it's important for parents to know the warning signs so teens who might be suicidal can get the help they need.

Some adults feel that kids who say they are going to hurt or kill themselves are "just doing it for attention." It's important to realize that if teens are ignored when seeking attention, it may increase the chance of them harming themselves (or worse).

Getting attention in the form of ER visits, doctor's appointments, and residential treatment generally is not something teens want—unless they're seriously depressed and thinking about suicide or at least wishing they were dead. It's important to see warning signs as serious, not as "attention-seeking" to be ignored.

Watch and Listen

Keep a close eye on a teen who is depressed and withdrawn. Understanding depression in teens is very important since it can look different from commonly held beliefs about depression. For example, it may take the form of problems with friends, grades, sleep, or being cranky and irritable rather than chronic sadness or crying.

It's important to try to keep the lines of communication open and express your concern, support, and love. If your teen confides in you, show that you take those concerns seriously. A fight with a friend might not seem like a big deal to you in the larger scheme of things, but for a teen it can feel immense and consuming. It's important not to minimize or discount what your teen is going through, as this can increase his or her sense of hopelessness.

If your teen doesn't feel comfortable talking with you, suggest a more neutral person, such as another relative, a clergy member, a coach, a school counselor, or your child's doctor.

Ask Questions

Some parents are reluctant to ask teens if they have been thinking about suicide or hurting themselves. Some fear that by asking, they will plant the idea of suicide in their teen's head.

It's always a good idea to ask, even though doing so can be difficult. Sometimes it helps to explain why you're asking. For instance, you might say: "I've noticed that you've been talking a lot about wanting to be dead. Have you been having thoughts about trying to kill yourself?"

Get Help

If you learn that your child is thinking about suicide, get help immediately. Your doctor can refer you to a psychologist or psychiatrist, or your local hospital's department of psychiatry can provide a list of doctors in your area. Your local mental health association or county medical society can also provide references. In an emergency, you can call *(800) SUICIDE.*

If your teen is in a crisis situation, your local emergency room can conduct a comprehensive psychiatric evaluation and refer you to the appropriate resources. If you're unsure about whether you should bring your child to the emergency room, contact your doctor or call (800) SUICIDE for help.

If you've scheduled an appointment with a mental health professional, make sure to keep the appointment, even if your teen says he or she is feeling better or doesn't want to go. Suicidal thoughts do tend to come and go; however, it is important that your teen get help developing the skills necessary to decrease the likelihood that suicidal thoughts and behaviors will emerge again if a crisis arises.

If your teen refuses to go to the appointment, discuss this with the mental health professional—and consider attending the session and working with the clinician to make sure your teen has access to the help needed. The clinician also might be able to help you devise strategies to help your teen want to get help.

Remember that ongoing conflicts between a parent and child can fuel the fire for a teen who is feeling isolated, misunderstood, devalued, or suicidal. Get help to air family problems and resolve them in a constructive way. Also let the mental health professional know if there is a history of depression, substance abuse, family violence, or other stresses at home, such as an ongoing environment of criticism.

Helping Teens Cope with Loss

What should you do if someone your teen knows, perhaps a family member, friend, or a classmate, has attempted or committed suicide? First, acknowledge your child's many emotions. Some teens say they feel guilty—especially those who felt they could have interpreted their friend's actions and words better.

Others say they feel angry with the person who committed or attempted suicide for having done something so selfish. Still others say they feel no strong emotions or don't know how to express how they feel. Reassure your child that there is no right or wrong way to feel, and that it's OK to talk about it when he or she feels ready.

When someone attempts suicide and survives, people might be afraid of or uncomfortable talking with him or her about it. Tell your teen to resist this urge; this is a time when a person absolutely needs to feel connected to others.

Many schools address a student's suicide by calling in special counselors to talk with the students and help them cope. If your teen is dealing with a friend or classmate's suicide, encourage him or her to make use of these resources or to talk to you or another trusted adult.

If You've Lost a Child to Suicide

For parents, the death of a child is the most painful loss imaginable. For parents who've lost a child to suicide, the pain and grief can be intensified. Although these feelings may never completely go away, survivors of suicide can take steps to begin the healing process:

- Maintain contact with others. Suicide can be a very isolating experience for surviving family members because friends often don't know what to say or how to help. Seek out supportive people to talk with about your child and your feelings. If those around you seem uncomfortable about reaching out, initiate the conversation and ask for their help.
- Remember that your other family members are grieving, too, and that everyone expresses grief in their own way. Your other children, in particular, may try to deal with their pain alone so as not to burden you with additional worries. Be there for each other through the tears, anger, and silences—and, if necessary, seek help and support together.
- Expect that anniversaries, birthdays, and holidays may be difficult. Important days and holidays often reawaken a sense of loss and anxiety. On those days, do what's best for your emotional needs, whether that means surrounding yourself with family and friends or planning a quiet day of reflection.
- Understand that it's normal to feel guilty and to question how this could have happened, but it's also important to realize that you might never get the answers you seek. The healing that takes place over time comes from reaching a point of forgiveness—for both your child and yourself.
- Counseling and support groups can play a tremendous role in helping you to realize you are not alone. Some bereaved family members become part of the suicide prevention network that helps parents, teenagers, and schools learn how to help prevent future tragedies.

Source: Kidshealth, "About Teen Suicide." Available at: http://kidshealth.org/parent/emotions/ behavior/suicide.html. Copyright © The Nemours Foundation/KidsHealth. Reprinted with permission.

"SUICIDE FACTS AT A GLANCE"

This helpful and complete fact sheet was assembled by the CDC (Centers for Disease Control), an organization that can access the best and most complete data sets available. Although there are few explanations or analyses, it is a good source for factual information. In general, the CDC is an excellent site for medical and health information, and uses language that is easily understood and is not too technical or "scientific" in their descriptions and discussions.

In addition to discussing suicide, this fact sheet also reviews "nonsuicidal thoughts and behavior," "gender disparities," "racial and ethnic disparities," "age group differences," and "nonfatal, self-inflicted injuries." While these facts are instructive, they do not analyze or conclude any general summaries. However, researchers can certainly use the facts and references that are included in order to draw their own conclusions and to stimulate further research. For a quick and accessible source of pure information, the CDC site is one of the best, but it will also refer the reader to additional helpful sites. However, if a person needs information in a crisis or urgent situation this might not be the best site to go to. Conversely, for the person who just wants factual information about suicide in a clear and very understandable way—this is an excellent site and one that is very trustworthy with respect to the accuracy and validity of the information.

Suicide
- Suicide was the tenth leading cause of death for all ages in 2010.[1]
- There were 38,364 suicides in 2010 in the United States—an average of 105 each day.[1]
- Based on data about suicides in 16 National Violent Death Reporting System states in 2009, 33.3% of suicide decedents tested positive for alcohol, 23% for antidepressants, and 20.8% for opiates, including heroin and prescription pain killers.[2]
- Suicide results in an estimated $34.6 billion in combined medical and work loss costs.[1]

Nonfatal Suicidal Thoughts and Behavior
- Among adults aged 18 years in the United States during 2008–2009:[3]
  - An estimated 8.3 million adults (3.7% of the adult U.S. population) reported having suicidal thoughts in the past year.
  - An estimated 2.2 million adults (1.0% of the adult U.S. population) reported having made suicide plans in the past year.
  - An estimated 1 million adults (0.5% of the U.S. adult population) reported making a suicide attempt in the past year.
- There is one suicide for every 25 attempted suicides.[3]
- Among young adults ages 15 to 24 years old, there are approximately 100–200 attempts for every completed suicide.[4]
- In a 2011 nationally-representative sample of youth in grades 9–12:[5]
  - 15.8% of students reported that they had seriously considered attempting suicide during the 12 months preceding the survey;

- 12.8% of students reported that they made a plan about how they would attempt suicide during the 12 months preceding the survey;
- 7.8% of students reported that they had attempted suicide one or more times during the 12 months preceding the survey; and
- 2.4% of students reported that they had made a suicide attempt that resulted in an injury, poisoning, or an overdose that required medical attention.

Gender Disparities

- Suicide among males is four times higher than among females and represents 79% of all U.S. suicides.[1]
- Females are more likely than males to have had suicidal thoughts.[3]
- Firearms are the most commonly used method of suicide among males (56%).[1]
- Poisoning is the most common method of suicide for females (37.4%).[1]

Racial and Ethnic Disparities

- Among American Indians/Alaska Natives aged 15- to 34-years, suicide is the second leading cause of death.[1]
- The suicide rate among American Indian/Alaska Native adolescents and young adults ages 15 to 34 (31 per 100,000) is 2.5 times higher than the national average for that age group (12.2 per 100,000).[1]
- Of students in grades 9–12, significantly more Hispanic female students (13.5%) reported attempting suicide in the last year than Black, non-Hispanic female students (8.8%) and White, non-Hispanic female students (7.9%).[5]

Age Group Differences

- Suicide is the third leading cause of death among persons aged 15–24 years, the second among persons aged 25–34 years, the fourth among person aged 35–54 years, and the eighth among person 55–64 years.[1]
- Among 15- to 24-year olds, suicide accounts for 20% of all deaths annually.[1]
- Suicide rates for females are highest among those aged 45–54 (rate 9 per 100,000 population).[1]
- Suicide rates for males are highest among those aged 75 and older (rate 36 per 100,000).[1]
- The rate of suicide for adults aged 75 years and older was 16.3 per 100,000.[1]
- The prevalence of suicidal thoughts, suicide planning, and suicide attempts is significantly higher among young adults aged 18–29 years than among adults aged <30 years.[3]

Nonfatal, Self-Inflicted Injuries*

- In 2011, 487,700 people were treated in emergency departments for self-inflicted injuries.[1]
- Nonfatal, self-inflicted injuries result in an estimated $6.5 billion in combined medical and work loss costs.[1]

REFERENCES

1. Centers for Disease Control and Prevention, National Center for Injury Prevention and Control. Web-based Injury Statistics Query and Reporting System (WISQARS) [online]. (2010). [cited 2012 Oct 19] Available at: www.cdc.gov/injury/wisqars/index. html.
2. Karch DL, Logan J, McDaniel D, Parks S, Patel N. Surveillance for violent deaths—National Violent Death Reporting System, 16 States, 2009. MMWR Surveillance Summary 2012; 61:1–43. Available at: http://www.cdc.gov/mmwr/preview/mmwrhtml/ ss6106a1.htm?s_cid=ss6106a1_e#tab6.
3. Crosby AE, Han B, Ortega LAG, Parks SE, Gfoerer J. Suicidal thoughts and behaviors among adults aged >18 years-United States, 2008–2009. MMWR Surveillance Summaries 2011; 60 (no. SS-13). Available at: www.cdc.gov/mmwr/preview/mmwrhtml/ss6013a1.htm?s_cid=ss6013a1_e.
4. Goldsmith SK, Pellmar TC, Kleinman AM, Bunney WE, editors. Reducing suicide: a national imperative. Washington, DC: National Academy Press; 2002.
5. Centers for Disease Control and Prevention. Youth risk behavior surveillance—United States, 2011. MMWR, Surveillance Summaries 2012; 61 (no. SS-4). Available at: www.cdc.gov/mmwr/pdf/ss/ss6104.pdf.

Source: Suicide Facts at a Glance, 2012. National Center for Injury Prevention and Control, Division of Violence Prevention, Centers for Disease Control. Available at: http://www.cdc.gov/violenceprevention/pdf/suicide_datasheet_2012-a.pdf.

---

* The term "self-inflicted injuries" refers to suicidal and nonsuicidal behaviors such as self-mutilation.

TIMELINE

Throughout history many important events related to the subject of suicide have occurred, and some have become famous due to the victim's political, legal, or social circumstances. The following timeline represents some of the more famous recorded suicides, and some events related to suicide politically, legally, socially, and medically.

399 BCE   Socrates, Greek philosopher, commits suicide. He was arrested for rejecting the gods acknowledged by the state, of introducing strange deities, and corrupting the youth. He "voluntarily" drank hemlock (a poison) in compliance with the state's directive.

2nd Century BCE   The Teutons marched through Gaul along with their neighbors the Cimbri, attacking Rome where they were defeated and their king captured and put in irons. Rather than submit to the Romans, the 300 married women who were turned over to the Romans slay their children and then commit suicide.

183–182 BCE   Hannibal, the Carthaginian general, commits suicide. Some say a comet in the night sky was an omen of his death.

133 BCE   After a 15-month siege by the Romans, most of the defeated Numantines set fire to the city and commit suicide, rather than surrender.

30 BCE   Rome gains control over Egypt and its wheat fields become Rome's major source of food. Cleopatra (pharaoh of Egypt) and her lover Marc Anthony (a Roman) commit suicide rather than face the Roman armies.

9 BCE Publius Quinctilius Varus, Roman viceroy of Syria, commits suicide at age 59 after losing a battle to the Germanic tribes in the north. He apparently wanted to avoid the shame and likely torture and execution by the Germanic armies.

68 CE Claudius Nero, Roman emperor commits suicide at age 31. He was known for his viciousness and extravagance and was believed to have "fiddled while Rome burned" because he wanted to clear land for the expansion of his palace; he believed (accurately as history records) that he was to be assassinated.

73 CE The 960 members of the Sicarii Jewish community at Masada collectively commit suicide rather than be conquered and enslaved by the Romans. Each man killed his wife and children, then the men drew lots and killed each other, until the last man killed himself.

Note: All of the following dates are in the Common Era (CE).

1303, 1535, and 1568 The practice of mass suicide called "Jauhar" was carried out by Indian women whenever the fall of a city by Muslim invaders was certain. Several recorded events prove that they chose suicide over dishonor.

1336 When the castle of Pilenai (in Lithuania) was besieged by Teutonic knights, the defenders led by Duke Margiris, realizing their futile situation, make the decision to commit mass suicide as well as set the castle on fire to keep anything of value from falling into enemy hands.

1575–1625 AD Members of the U'wa tribe, in what is now Columbia, South America, throw themselves off of a cliff in protest of Spanish colonialism and occupation.

1644 Two hundred members of the Peking imperial family/court (last of the Ming Dynasty) commit suicide after the city was taken by rebel forces.

1644 Si Sang, last Ming emperor of China commits suicide along with many of his family and followers.

17th Century Common Law tradition prohibits suicide and assisted suicide in the American Colonies. This law was one of the first legal precedents in North America.

1828 The earliest American statute explicitly outlawing assisting suicide is enacted in New York.

October 11, 1878 Kiowa leader Santanta, known as the "Orator of the Plains," surrenders to authorities in Darlington, Texas, is sent to prison, and commits suicide.

1906–1908	Mass suicides in Bali, with a ritual called a "puputan," are committed rather than submitting to the overwhelming Dutch colonial forces.
November 13, 1937	Edward Wutke, a convicted murderer serving a 27-year sentence, is the first person to commit suicide at Alcatraz Prison.
1942	Switzerland passes a euthanasia law to enable those with just a few weeks to live the opportunity of a dignified death. Swiss law makes assisted suicide lawful under some conditions.
October 14, 1944	Erwin Rommel, Nazi Field Marshall, dies by taking a cyanide pill. It is believed that he was ordered to commit suicide or face a court martial for plotting against Hitler.
1945	A number of Nazis commit suicide rather than face a war crimes tribunal, including Adolph Hitler, German dictator; Heinrich Himmler, Gestapo leader; Paul Josef Goebbels, Minister of Propaganda; Eva Braun, mistress/wife of Hitler; Walter Model, Nazi field marshal; and Gunther von Kluge, Nazi field marshal.
May 1, 1945	About 1,000 residents of Demmin, Germany, commit mass suicide after the Red Army sacks the town. They feared how they would be treated by the Soviet troops.
June 1945	The Japanese army, facing an impending U.S. invasion, hands out grenades to residents in Okinawa and orders them to kill themselves rather than surrender to the Americans; over 500 commit suicide.
September 8, 1945	Hideki Tojo, Japanese prime minister, attempts suicide rather than face a war crimes tribunal but is unsuccessful and is later hanged on December 23, 1948.
August 3, 1961	Britain's Parliament adopts the Suicide Act of 1961, which decriminalizes suicide in the United Kingdom, but makes assisting a suicide punishable by up to 14 years in jail.
1961	Ernest Hemmingway dies by a shotgun blast to his head. Although his wife and others assert that it was an accident, it is widely believed to be a suicide due to his failing health, fears, and suspicions about the government spying on him, and other concerns. His suicide is often presented as a glamorous choice by a desperate man.
August 5, 1962	Marilyn Monroe is found dead in her bedroom from a barbiturate overdose, and it is ruled a "probable suicide." Many believe that she was murdered, while others feel that it was an accident. It does however, lead to an increase in suicides by others during that period.

1968   Dr. Robert Schuller founds New Hope, the first Christian 24-hour suicide-prevention center.

1973   The American Hospital Association adopts a "Patient's Bill of Rights," which recognizes a patient's right to refuse treatment.

November 18, 1978   In Jonestown, Guyana, Rep. Leo J. Ryan and four other people investigating the Jim Jones cult are killed by members of the People's Temple. That same night there were more killings and mass suicides, including the "Reverend" Jim Jones. Ultimately, 918 people die, including 260 children.

1980   Derek Humphrey forms the "Hemlock Society" in California, a grassroots organization supporting euthanasia and assisted suicide.

April 18, 1983   At the U.S. embassy in Beirut, Lebanon, 63 people including 17 U.S. citizens are killed by a suicide bomber. Although this is not the first suicide bomber, it attracts much media attention, only to be followed by hundreds of similar incidents over the years and until the present time all around the world.

1985   A jury in New Jersey rules that terminally ill patients have the right to starve themselves.

August 20, 1986   Postal employee Patrick Henry Sherrill goes on a deadly rampage at a post office in Edmond, Oklahoma, shooting and killing 14 fellow workers before killing himself. Although the post office remains a safe place to work, this event is credited with inspiring the phrase, "going postal."

1987   The California State Bar Conference becomes the first major public body to support physician aid in dying.

August 17, 1987   Rudolf Hess, the last member of Hitler's inner circle, apparently kills himself at age 93 in Spandau Prison; his family claims it was murder.

1988   The Unitarian Universalist Association passes a resolution in support of aid in dying.

June 4, 1990   Dr. Jack Kevorkian participates in his first assisted suicide in Michigan. The patient, Janet Adkins, was a Hemlock Society member.

June 25, 1990   The Supreme Court rules that a person has the right to refuse lifesaving medical treatment.

November 5, 1990   Congress passes the Patient Self-Determination Act, requiring hospitals that receive federal funds to tell patients that they have the right to demand or refuse treatment.

February 5, 1991	A Michigan court bars Dr. Jack Kevorkian from assisting in suicides.
October 23, 1991	Dr. Jack Kevorkian attends the suicide machine assisted deaths of two women in Michigan.
November 1991	Michigan suspends the medical license of Dr. Kevorkian.
December 17, 1993	Dr. Kevorkian is released from jail in Oakland County, Michigan, after promising not to help anyone end their life.
April 5, 1994	Singer/musician Kurt Cobain of the band Nirvana commits suicide in Seattle, Washington. Although he is one of a number of celebrities who killed themselves, his death was particularly influential among his fans and followers and served to glamourize suicide among these groups.
March 8, 1996	Dr. Jack Kevorkian is acquitted of assisted suicide for helping two suffering patients kill themselves.
April 2, 1996	A federal appeals court rejects New York state laws banning doctor-assisted suicide, saying it would be discriminatory to let people disconnect life-support systems, while refusing to let others end their life with medication.
May 14, 1996	A jury in Pontiac, Michigan, acquits Dr. Jack Kevorkian of assisted suicide charges, his third legal victory in two years. The judge dismisses murder charges in the same case.
September 7, 1996	Isabel Correa becomes the 40th person known to die in the presence of Dr. Kevorkian, less than a day after police burst into a Michigan motel room, interrupting a meeting between her and Kevorkian.
September 22, 1996	In Australia, Bob Dent becomes the first person to kill himself legally under the new voluntary euthanasia law.
October 31, 1996	In Pontiac, Michigan, Dr. Jack Kevorkian is charged with assisting three suicides since June 1996; he is later acquitted.
March 22, 1997	In Canada, five Solar Temple cult members die in an apparent mass suicide in Quebec, one of a number of cult-related suicides in various countries.
March 24, 1997	The Australian Senate strikes down the law that allows doctor-assisted suicides for the terminally ill.
March 26, 1997	The bodies of 39 young men and women of the Heaven's Gate cult are discovered, the apparent result of a mass suicide. With the approach of the Hale-Bopp comet, they believed that the "End of Days" was near.

April 21, 1997   A federal court blocks Oregon's 1994 approved law on doctor-assisted suicide.

June 26, 1997   The U.S. Supreme Court rules that terminally ill U.S. citizens have no constitutional right to doctor-assisted suicide, but do nothing to bar individual states from legalizing the process.

November 22, 1998   The CBS program *60 Minutes* shows a videotape of Dr. Jack Kevorkian giving lethal drugs to Thomas Youk, a terminally ill patient. Dr. Kevorkian challenges prosecutors to arrest him; he is later sentenced to up to 25 years for second-degree murder.

1998   In Oregon, 15 terminally ill people take advantage of the new assisted suicide law.

March 22, 1999   Acting as his own attorney, Dr. Jack Kevorkian goes on trial for murder charges, and for the first time tells a jury in Pontiac, Michigan, that he was merely carrying out his professional duty in the videotape of the assisted suicide on CBS's *60 Minutes.* Although charged with first-degree murder, he is convicted of second-degree murder.

July 28, 1999   U.S. Surgeon General David Satcher declares suicide a serious national threat.

March 17, 2000   The 778 deaths of members of the Ugandan group "Movement for the Restoration of the Ten Commandments of God" is considered a mass murder and suicide orchestrated by the leaders of the group.

April 17, 2002   U.S. district judge Robert Jones upholds Oregon's assisted-suicide law and says that Attorney General John Ashcroft should not "determine the legitimacy" of medical acts.

April 2005   The Council of Europe, Europe's top human rights body, rejects euthanasia as a legitimate means to end life.

April 27, 2006   A Dutch agency reports that the number of cases of legal euthanasia and doctor-assisted suicide has increased in 2005 for the third straight year.

June 29, 2006   Delegates to the annual conference of the British Medical Association vote against the legalization of doctor-assisted suicide and voluntary euthanasia in Britain.

December 22, 2006   The Roman Catholic Church denies a religious funeral for Piergiogio Welby, the paralyzed Italian author, who dies after a doctor disconnected his respirator, saying that it would treat his public wish to "end his life" as a willful suicide.

February 2, 2007 A ruling by Switzerland's highest court opens the possibility that people with serious mental illnesses can be assisted by doctors to end their life.

June 1, 2007 Dr. Jack Kevorkian is released from prison on parole after serving eight years.

September 29, 2007 In southern Japan more than 100,000 people protest against the central government's order to modify school textbooks that say the country's army forced civilians to commit mass suicide at the end of World War II.

March 19, 2008 Chantal Sebire, who suffered from a painful facial tumor, is found dead. Her quest for a doctor-assisted suicide generated headlines across France. Two days before, a court in the city of Dijon had rejected her wish for doctor-assisted suicide.

November 4, 2008 Washington becomes the second state after Oregon to legalize assisted suicide.

December 6, 2008 A Montana state judge rules that doctor-assisted suicides are legal in that state.

July 25, 2009 In Britain a new poll is released showing solid support for the right to die. The Royal College of Nursing says it is adopting a neutral stance on the issue after its research showed that nurses were divided. The British Medical Association remained opposed.

August 14, 2009 An Australian judge rules that Christian Rossiter, a quadriplegic man who stated that he could not fulfill normal human functions, has the right to instruct the nursing home in which he lived to stop feeding him and allow him to die. He dies on September 21, 2009.

September 23, 2009 England's top prosecutor unveils new guidelines that could decriminalize many forms of assisted suicide, saying that most people who help close friends or family kill themselves are not likely to face charges.

December 31, 2009 The Montana Supreme Court says that nothing in state law prevents patients from seeking physician-assisted suicide, making Montana the third state to allow the procedure.

February 25, 2010 Prosecutors in England and Wales receive fresh guidelines on assisted suicide that reduce the likelihood that helping a loved one commit suicide will result in charges being filed.

June 24, 2010 Germany's Supreme Court issues a landmark ruling that an assisted suicide cannot be punished if it is carried out based on a patient's prior request.

June 3, 2011   Dr. Jack Kevorkian, a champion for doctor-assisted suicide, dies at age 83 from complications of kidney disease and pneumonia in a hospital in Royal Oaks, Michigan.

October 28, 2011   India's government says that the rate of suicides in India is increasing and that more than 15 people kill themselves every hour.

January 27, 2012   A paralyzed British man who wanted to die wins the first round in his legal battle when the high court rules that his lawyers won't be prosecuted if they seek outside experts to help him commit suicide.

March 27, 2012   Swiss authorities say that 5 out of every 1,000 deaths in Switzerland now involve assisted suicide, with women more likely to choose this form of death than men.

May 9, 2012   Argentina's senate overwhelmingly approves a "dignified death" law, giving terminally ill patients and their families more power to make end-of-life decisions; it passes the lower house last year.

June 8, 2012   Pentagon statistics shows that 154 suicides among active-duty troops in the first 155 days of the year far outdistance the number of U.S. forces members killed in action in Afghanistan—about 50 percent more.

June 15, 2012   A British Columbia Supreme Court justice in Canada rules that federal laws banning assisted suicide are unconstitutional because they discriminate against severely ill patients.

August 16, 2012   British high court judges dismiss a legal plea by Tony Nicklinson for the right to die, unanimously ruling that it would be wrong to depart from a precedent that equates voluntary euthanasia with murder. He dies in his home on August 22, 2012, after contracting pneumonia.

April 29, 2013   Ireland's Supreme Court rules that a paralyzed Irish woman, who wanted to die, cannot legally commit suicide with her partner's help. Judges say that lawmakers can pass such a law to permit Marie Fleming to die at a time of her choosing, but no such statute yet existed.

May 14, 2013   The European Court of Human rights finds that Swiss laws on passive assisted suicide are unclear and need revising to clarify when people are entitled to a medical prescription for a lethal dose of drugs.

September 24, 2013 In the Netherlands the commission that examines euthanasia cases says that such cases rose by 13 percent in 2012 from 2011, the sixth consecutive year of increases; 4,188 cases were recorded in 2012.

GLOSSARY

Acute: Something (like an illness or psychological problem) that has a sudden onset or quick increase in symptoms that warrants urgent attention.

Addiction: A compulsive need for and use of a habit-forming substance that involves increased tolerance for the substance and well-defined symptoms of withdrawal when the use of the substance is stopped.

Adrenalin junkies: People who depend upon and need to engage in high-risk activities for their arousal and excitement.

AlAnon: A voluntary program based on the Twelve-Step heritage (e.g., Alcoholics Anonymous) that is intended to provide support and education for friends and family of someone dealing with substance addiction.

ALS: Amyotrophic lateral sclerosis, a chronic and debilitating neuromuscular disease that is typically fatal; also called "Lou Gehrig Disease" after the famous baseball player, of the New York Yankees, who died from this condition.

Altruistic suicide: Suicide that is performed to protect one's honor for themselves and their family (e.g., hara-kiri).

Angels of Death: People who undertake euthanasia for the purpose of ending the life of a patient who is in constant pain and/or who has no apparent quality of life. This is usually done without the consent of the patient.

Anomic suicide: A type of suicide identified by Emile Durkheim that is committed when a person experiences a marked disruption in their life; for example, losing a job, home, or family member.

Antibiotics: Medications that are used to treat infections caused by bacteria.

Antidepressant medications: Medications that are used to treat depression.

Anxiety disorder: A psychological disorder that is characterized by experiencing clinically relevant and severe anxiety. Different anxiety disorders depend upon the symptoms of the specific disorder, but all of the symptoms are anxiety based.

Assisted suicide: Suicide that is committed with the help of another person. For example, if a patient wants to end their life but is too infirm to actually accomplish the act, they ask someone else to do something that will result in the patient's death.

Bipolar disoruer: A serious mood disorder that is characterized by both depression and mania. This is not just "moodiness" but involves clinically serious symptoms that are disruptive to the person's life and that usually create distress for the patient. This used to be called "manic-depressive disorder."

Black Box Warning: Warnings that are placed on certain medications with precautions about their use and risks. This warning is imposed by the Food and Drug Administration, and must be placed on each box or informational insert of the medication.

Brain dead: When a patient who is still alive but has no apparent brain activity of a meaningful nature. There would be no evidence of consciousness or other higher mental functions and no expectation that these functions would ever be recovered.

Buddhism: A religion of eastern and central Asia growing out of the teachings of Gautama Buddha that centers on the belief that suffering is inherent in life and that one can be liberated from it by mental and moral self-purification.

Bullycide: When a person commits suicide because they have been the victim of serious bullying at the hands of other people.

Chronic: Something occurring over a long term and develops slowly or continues to occur frequently. As opposed to "acute," "chronic" refers to a condition that develops gradually and does not go away.

Clerics: Members of the clergy from any religion.

Commitment: Legal commitment involves the court ordering a person be held in a treatment facility for evaluation and/or treatment without the agreement of the person involved. They can be held against their will for as long as the court deems necessary.

Competence: Legal competence means that a person has the capacity to make decisions for themselves (e.g., sign contracts, vote, make medical decisions, and manage their own funds). In addition, people can be judged to be incompetent to stand trial. Being competent to stand trial means that they understand the nature and quality of the act in question, and that they can participate in their own defense.

Confidentiality: An understanding or agreement that something known about or said/written by or about a person will not be shared or released without the knowledge and permission of the person in question.

Copycat suicide: When a person commits suicide because another person (usually famous) commits suicide.

Counselor: Anyone who counsels or gives advice to another person. A mental health counselor provides support and advice to people suffering from mental health conditions. These are not necessarily professionals licensed in professions such as psychology, psychiatry, or social work. Some states provide licensing for mental health counselors as an independent profession.

Delusion: A persistent false, abnormal belief regarding the self or persons/objects outside the self that is maintained despite indisputable evidence to the contrary; *also,* the abnormal state is marked by such beliefs.

Depression: A mood disorder that is characterized by sadness, lack of energy and motivation, sleep difficulties, lack of pleasure in usually rewarding activities, physical symptoms, and feelings of helplessness and hopelessness.

Diagnosis: The investigation or analysis of the cause or nature of a condition, situation, or problem; the art or act of identifying a disease from its signs and symptoms.

Discrimination: Acting in ways to treat certain people or groups differently because of their membership or identification with a specific group, race, ethnicity, religion, among others. This treatment is also to the disadvantage of the person or group affected.

Disinhibiting effect: The effect produced by certain substances (e.g., alcohol), which reduces the likelihood that a person will inhibit the behaviors that they would normally not engage in.

DNR: See "Do Not Resuscitate."

Do Not Resuscitate: A medical order signed by a patient or their guardian or legal representative that states that the patient does not want "heroic means" undertaken to revive them after they have died.

Egoistic suicide: A type of suicide identified by Emile Durkheim when a person loses social supports and cannot face things alone.

Electroconvulsive therapy (ECT): A type of medical treatment (that may be used to treat severe depression) where electric currents are passed through the brain and produce convulsions; today, medications are used so that the patients do not demonstrate the convulsions, although the brain responds as if a seizure were occurring.

Epidemiology: A branch of medical science that deals with the incidence, distribution, and control of disease in a population.

Ethnic: Related to a large group of people who share common racial, linguistic, cultural, historical, and other characteristics.

Euthanasia: The practice of killing or permitting the death of hopelessly sick or injured individuals (such as persons or domestic animals) in a relatively painless way for reasons of mercy and to relieve them from suffering.

Family therapy: Psychotherapy that is conducted with a family unit for the purpose of helping the family deal with issues that are presenting problems for them.

Fatalistic suicide: A type of suicide when a person loses control over their own destiny; for example, a suicide is initiated/facilitated by membership in a cult.

Grief: A deep sadness and distress caused by a significant loss; for example, the death of a loved one.

Hallucinations: Perception-like experiences when a person misinterprets internal or subtle external stimuli as true perceptions; for example, hearing "voices" or seeing a "vision."

Hara-kiri: Ritualistic Japanese suicide that involves self-disembowelment with a knife, usually performed to save face for the person or his family.

Health Care Proxy: A person who is given the responsibility for making medical decisions on behalf of a patient when or if the patient does not have the capacity to make the decision themselves. A document is signed by the patient in the presence of a witness while they are still competent to make that decision.

Hinduism: The dominant religion of India, which includes the worship of many gods and the belief that after you die, you return to life in a different form.

Hispanic: Having to do with a person originally coming from an area where Spanish is spoken, especially Latin America; also, of or relating to Hispanic people.

Homicide: The killing of a person or persons by another person or persons.

Hospice: A program of care for terminally ill patients and their families. Care is often provided in the patient's home but can also be in a hospital or other facility. It is a multidisciplinary program intended to meet the medical, social, personal, and spiritual needs of patients and their families.

Hypothermia: A condition where the body temperature is abnormally low. If this condition lasts too long, it can be fatal.

Immolation: A deliberate and willful sacrifice by setting oneself on fire.

Impulse control disorder: A psychological condition when a person has difficulties because of their inability to control their impulses; for example, gambling, aggression, theft, among others.

Insanity: A severe mental illness that involves a deranged state of mind usually occurring as a specific disorder (e.g., schizophrenia). Legally, unsoundness of mind or lack of understanding can prevent a person from having the mental capacity required by law to enter into a particular relationship, status, or transaction, or can remove a person from criminal or civil responsibility.

Internet: An electronic communications network that connects computer networks and organizational computer facilities around the world.

Involuntary commitment: A court orders an individual to be committed to a mental health treatment facility against their will for evaluation and/or treatment. The commitment is typically for a specified period of time and must be reevaluated if the doctors believe that the person needs to remain in the facility.

Involuntary euthanasia: Also call "mercy killing," where a person kills another person who is suffering from a hopeless condition, but is performed without the knowledge or agreement of the patient/victim.

Irrational suicide: A suicide that was judged by others to "not make sense," to be regretful, capricious, and harmful to the victim.

Islamic: Having to do with the religion of Islam, which teaches that there is only one God (Allah) and that Muhammad is God's prophet; this is the religion of Muslims.

Jainism: A religion primarily of India that originated in the sixth century BCE and teaches liberation of the soul by right knowledge, right faith, and right conduct.

Jauhar: The occasional practice of mass suicide carried out in medieval times by women of the Rajput communities in India, when the fall of a city besieged by Muslim invaders was certain, in order to avoid capture and dishonor.

Kamikazee: One of a group of Japanese pilots in World War II who were assigned to crash their planes into targets such as ships. These were considered to be "suicide missions" since the pilots rarely survived. "Kamikazee" is translated as "divine wind."

Living Will: A document in which a person says what medical decisions should be made if they become too sick or injured to make those decisions. Typically, in this document the signer requests to be allowed to die rather than be kept alive by artificial means if disabled beyond a reasonable expectation of recovery.

Manic-depressive disease: See "Bipolar disorder."

Mass suicide: Suicide committed by a large group of people at approximately the same time and for the same or similar reasons.

Medical ethicist: A person who studies and practices medical ethics, a system of moral principles that applies values and judgments to the practice of medicine. As a scholarly discipline, medical ethics encompasses its practical application in clinical settings, and works on its history, philosophy, theology, and sociology.

Mental Status Exam: An important part of the clinical assessment process in psychiatric and psychological practice. It is a structured way of observing and describing a patient's current state of mind under the domains of appearance, attitude, behavior, mood and affect, speech, thought process, thought content, perception, cognition, insight, and judgment.

Mercy killing: See "Euthanasia."

Mortality rate: A measure of the number of deaths in general, or due to a specific cause, in a population, scaled to the size of that population, per unit of time. Mortality rate is typically expressed in units of deaths per 1,000 individuals per year.

Motives: The reason why someone performs a particular act or behaves in certain ways, usually based on needs, goals, or desires. Sometimes motives are clear and obvious but often they are based on factors that may not be observable or even conscious.

Murder-suicide: A person murders another person or persons and then takes their own life.

Negligence: The failure to demonstrate responsible care or the lack of normal care or attention; the state produced by neglect.

Nonvoluntary euthanasia: Similar to mercy killing where someone kills or causes the death of another person because they feel that the person's life is so filled with pain and suffering it would best for them to die. This is done without the awareness and/or consent of the patient in question. Sometimes the word "euthanasia" is used generically to include both voluntary and nonvoluntary situations.

Online: When a person is connected to a computer, a network, or the Internet.

Palliative care: A type of medical care where the goal of care is patient comfort and pain relief rather than cure. Unlike hospice care, patients in palliative care do not have to be suffering from a terminal disease with a limited life expectancy.

Passive suicide: A person has the *intention* of killing themselves, but rather than acting directly, they engage in behaviors that they expect will end their life prematurely at some point in the future. Not all people who engage in such action are passively suicidal—suicide implies the *intent* to do something that will cause death to the person in question.

Patriotic suicide: A person kills themselves "for the state" rather than face dishonor or bring dishonor on the state.

Personhood: The condition of being a person. This is a gender-free way of describing the quality of being a human being rather than saying either "manhood" or "womanhood."

Prayopavesa: In Sanskrit means "resolving to die through fasting"; this is a practice in Hinduism that denotes the suicide by a person fasting-starvation who has no desire or ambition, and no responsibilities remaining in life. It is also allowed in cases of terminal disease or great disability. A similar practice exists in Jainism, termed Santhara.

Prejudice: Literally "prejudging," where a person holds an attitude (usually negative) about a person or group that is not based in fact or reality, but rather on the person's preexisting beliefs and expectations about the person or group in question.

Prevention: Taking an action to try to avoid a particular outcome that is not desired.

Primary care physician (PCP): Usually a person's "main doctor," to whom a person would go for routine care such as an annual physical or for the treatment of common illnesses or conditions that would not require the care of a specialist.

Primary prevention: This is prevention that targets an entire population and is intended to reduce the incidence or occurrence of some condition in the entire population.

Prioritization: The setting of priorities; refers to a process where a list of related elements are arranged in terms of relative importance and/or urgency.

Prognosis: The prospect of recovery as anticipated from the usual course of disease or peculiarities of the case and the characteristics of the patient.

Psychiatrist: A physician who has completed medical school and has earned an MD or a DO, who does a residency to specialize in psychiatry, a specialty area that is concerned with the diagnosis and treatment of mental illness and related conditions. The psychiatrist typically uses psychotropic drugs to treat mental conditions.

Psychological autopsy: An evaluation performed to assess the mental condition of the victim prior to their death. This is often done in cases of apparent suicide to determine if there was a relevant motive why the person wanted to die.

Psychologist: A doctoral level specialist who has completed a PhD, PSYD, an EdD, or other relevant doctoral degree in the field of psychology. To be licensed to practice psychology in most states, a candidate is required to complete the doctoral degree from an accredited school, have an accredited internship, plus two years of supervised training and experience beyond their degree. Many psychologists also complete a postdoctoral fellowship to further specialize in a specific field. They usually rely on nonmedical types of treatment, such as psychotherapy to treat mental conditions. In some states and in the Department of Defense, some psychologists with additional training can also prescribe medications.

Psychosis: A fundamental derangement of the mind (as in schizophrenia) characterized by defective or loss of contact with reality, especially by delusions, hallucinations, and disorganized speech and behavior.

Psychosocial treatments: Types of treatments for mental conditions that rely primarily on psychological and social methods; for example, psychotherapy, group therapy, family therapy, among others.

Psychotherapy: Treatment of mental or emotional illness that relies on verbally and/or behaviorally based treatment methods rather than medical treatments, such as use of drugs.

Psychotropic drugs: Medications that are used for the treatment of psychological/mental conditions.

Racial: Relating to or based on race. Race refers to categories of humankind that share certain distinctive physical traits; a class or kind of people unified by shared interests, habits, or characteristics.

Rational suicide: A suicide that is judged by others to "make sense," to be positive and desired, carefully planned, and beneficial to the victim.

Red Guard: A paramilitary youth organization in China in the 1960s.

Reincarnation: The idea or belief that people are born again with a different body after death.

Revenge suicide: Committed with the intent to harm another person; it may involve a person killing themselves causing another person to feel guilty or distressed about the suicide.

Risk assessment: A process to determine the degree to which a given condition or situation is risky or has an uncertain outcome.

Ritual suicide: A suicide that is part of a tradition or ritual which a person is expected to fulfill under certain conditions. For example, warriors committing suicide after losing a battle rather than facing the humiliation of defeat, or a person in Japan committing *hara-kiri* (ritual self-disembowelment) to save face.

Samurai warrior: Historically, a member of the warrior aristocracy in Japan, who was highly trained and bound by strict conditions and expectations.

Santhara: See "Prayopavesa."

Sati: The Indian practice of a woman throwing herself on the funeral pyre of her husband or burning herself to death following her husband's death. It is based on the story of the goddess Sati, who burned herself to death in a fire she created with her yogic powers after her father insulted her husband, the god Shiva.

Schizophrenia: A psychotic disorder (serious mental illness) characterized by loss of contact with reality, noticeable deterioration in the level of functioning in everyday life, and a disintegration of personality, expressed as a disorder of feeling, thought (as delusions), perception (as hallucinations), and behavior.

Secondary prevention: A prevention program that targets a high-risk group in a population. For example, a suicide-prevention program that focuses on people who have a history of depression.

Self-harm: Anything that a person does to hurt themselves; it usually involves physical damage, such as superficial cutting, but also includes more serious acts that could result in the person's death.

Seppuku: See "Hara-kiri."

Significant other: This usually refers to one's life partner. This could be a spouse or another domestic partner with whom one's life is shared; these relationships usually involve people living together as a couple.

Social worker: A person who is trained to provide a range of mental health, social, and family treatments. Social work programs involve a two-year master's degree resulting in the master of social work (MSW) degree. A social worker, who works with mental health patients, is usually a clinical social worker (CSW); if the person is licensed to provide services, they would be a licensed clinical social worker (LCSW).

Sophist: A class of ancient Greek teachers of rhetoric, philosophy, and the art of successful living; prominent in the middle of the fifth century BCE. They were known for their adroit, subtle, and allegedly often misleading reasoning.

Stoics: A member of a school of philosophy founded by Zeno of Citium about 300 BCE (http://www.merriam-webster.com/dictionary/b.c.) holding that the wise man should be free from passion, unmoved by joy or grief, and submissive to natural law (http://www.merriam-webster.com/dictionary/natural law).

Suicidal ideation: Refers to a person thinking about suicide—especially their own death by suicide.

Suicidal intention: A condition where a person is not just thinking about suicide, but has planned it and "intends" to complete the act.

Suicidality: Refers to anything related to suicide; for example, thoughts, feelings, plans, intentions, attempts, or commission.

Suicide: The active and intentional taking of one's own life by one's own hand, or when the victim enlists the help of another person to take action to end the life of the victim.

Suicide attack: A person attacks another person or group knowing full well that the outcome of such an attack will be their own death. This is not the same thing as a person in the military participating in a "suicide mission," because the goal of that mission is not for the person to die.

Suicide by "accident": This refers to a situation when a person stages an "accident" that is really not an accident, but is intended to result in the person's death.

Suicide by cop: Occasionally, someone who is facing law-enforcement personnel will intentionally charge or fire at a police officer, following a warning to drop their weapon. The officer(s) must then take action (sometimes lethal) and possibly kill the attacker in order to protect themselves and/or the public.

Suicide by pact: An unusual situation where two or more people agree that, under specific circumstances, all of the people involved will commit suicide. Unlike mass suicide, victims are not usually pressured by the leader or a peer to participate; it is an understanding that binds people to the mutually agreed upon promise to commit suicide when certain conditions emerge.

Suicide contract: An agreement made by some mental health or health care providers with a patient where the person will not attempt suicide before contacting their provider first and giving them a chance to develop an alternative plan.

Support groups: People who get together to support one another and to learn from each other about particular issues or problems that they all share. For example, there are support groups in many communities for people who have survived suicide attempts, and also groups for family members or friends who have had someone close to them attempt or commit suicide.

Symptom: A change in a physical or mental process that indicates that an underlying disease or condition exists.

Tertiary prevention: This type of prevention targets people who have already experienced a disease or condition; the prevention is based on the need to minimize the negative effects of the condition and/or to try to keep it from happening again. An example would be a program to help survivors of a suicide attempt refrain from trying it again.

Therapist: A person who conducts therapy on a patient or client. Although this could be any type of therapy, it usually refers to a mental health therapist, who provides treatment for psychological/emotional/personal types of problems.

Trauma: A very difficult or unpleasant experience that causes someone to have mental or emotional problems, often for a long time. Medically this can refer to a serious injury to a person's body.

Voluntary death: A person chooses to die at a particular time, but as opposed to suicide, voluntary death is helpful to the patient, rational, well planned, and admirable.

Voluntary euthanasia: A situation where a patient asks for or agrees to have someone else take an action that will result in the patient's death; for example, giving a fatal dose of a medication or unplugging a lifesaving piece of equipment.

Werther effect: From the novel *The Sorrows of Young Werther* written by Goethe in 1774. Young Werther commits suicide by shooting himself after having been rejected by his "true love"; also called a "copycat suicide."

RESOURCES

SUICIDE WEBSITES

American Association of Suicidality: http://www.suicidology.org/home.
American Foundation for Suicide Prevention: http://www.afsp.org/understanding-suicide.
American Psychiatric Association: http://www.psychiatry.org/home/search-results ?k=suicide.
American Psychological Association: Suicide. http://www.apa.org/topics/suicide/.
MedlinePlus: http://www.nlm.nih.gov/medlineplus/suicide.html.
Mental Health America: Suicide. http://www.mentalhealthamerica.net/suicide.
Psychology Today: http://www.psychologytoday.com/basics/suicide.
Suicide Prevention Resource Center: http://www.sprc.org/WebMD—Depression Health Center; Recognizing the Warning Signs of Suicide: http://www .webmd.com/depression/guide/depression-recognizing-signs-of-suicide.
World Health Organization—Suicide: http://www.who.int/topics/suicide/en/.

SUICIDE BOOKS AND JOURNALS

Archives of Suicide Research. A journal published by the International Academy of Suicide Research, and all articles are relevant to the topic of suicide.
Fine, Carla. (1997). *No Time to Say Goodbye: Surviving the Suicide of a Loved One.* New York: Broadway Books.
Jamison, Kay Redfield. (1999). *Night Falls Fast: Understanding Suicide.* New York: Alfred A. Knopf.
Joiner, Thomas. (2005). *Why People Die by Suicide.* Cambridge, MA: Harvard University Press.
Lukas, Christopher and Seiden, Henry M. (2007). *Silent Grief: Living in the Wake of Suicide.* London: Jessica Kingsley Publishers.

Minois, George and Cochrane, Lydia G. (1999). *History of Suicide: Voluntary Death in Western Culture.* Baltimore, MD: Johns Hopkins University Press.

Runyon, Brent. (2005). *The Burn Journals.* New York: Vintage Press.

Salomon, Ron, and Christine Collins. (2007). *Suicide.* London, UK: Chelsea House.

Suicide and Life Threatening Behavior. A journal published by the American Association of Suicidology, and all of the articles in this journal are relevant to the topic of suicide and self-harm.

Williams, Heidi. (2009). *Teen Suicide.* Farmington Hills, MI: Greenhaven Press.

SUICIDE ARTICLES

Anderson, Scott. "The Urge to End It All." *New York Times Magazine,* June 6, 2008. Available at: http://www.nytimes.com/2008/07/06/magazine/06suicide-t.html?pagewanted=all&_r=0.

Burleigh, Nina. "Sexting, Shame and Suicide." *Rolling Stone Culture,* September 17, 2013. Available at: http://www.rollingstone.com/culture/news/sexting-shame-and-suicide-20130917.

Crouse, Janet Shaw. (2014). "Sad Truths about Teen Suicide." *American Thinker.* January 14, 2014. Available at: http://www.americanthinker.com/2014/01/sad_truths_about_teen_suicide.html.

Dokoupil, Tony. (2013). "The Suicide Epidemic." *Newsweek,* May 22, 2013. Available at: http://mag.newsweek.com/2013/05/22/why-suicide-has-become-and-epidemic-and-what-we-can-do-to-help.html.

"The Golden Suicides." *Vanity Fair,* 2008. Available at: http://www.vanityfair.com/culture/features/2008/01/suicides200801.

Høifødt, T. S., and Talseth, A-G. (2006). "Dealing with Suicidal Patients—A Challenging Task: A Qualitative Study of Young Physicians' Experiences." *BMC Medical Education,* 6:44. Available at: http://www.biomedcentral.com/1472–6920/6/44.

Kingley, Kim. (2013). "The Suicide Detective." *New York Times Magazine.* June 26, 2013. Available at: http://www.nytimes.com/2013/06/30/magazine/the-suicide-detective.html?pagewanted=all&_r=0.

Klomek, Anat Brunstein, Sourander, Andre, and Gould, Madelyn S. (2011). "Bullying and Suicide." *Psychiatric Times.* Available at: http://www.psychiatrictimes.com/suicide/bullying-and-suicide.

Parker, Ian. (2012). "The Story of a Suicide." *The New Yorker,* February 6, 2012. Available at: http://www.newyorker.com/reporting/2012/02/06/120206 fa_fact_parker.

"Teen Suicide." *The American Academy of Child & Adolescent Psychiatry:* http://www.aacap.org/AACAP/Families_and_Youth/Facts_for_Families/Facts_for_Families_Pages/Teen_Suicide_10.aspx.

INDEX

ABOUT THE AUTHOR

Rudy Nydegger, PhD, is professor of management and psychology at the School of Management at Union Graduate College and in the Department of Psychology at Union College, Schenectady, New York. He is a board-certified clinical psychologist with a private practice and consulting firm. In addition, he is chief of psychology at Ellis Hospital in Schenectady, New York. Former positions include assistant professor of psychology at Rice University, clinical assistant professor at Baylor College of Medicine, and adjunct professor at Cornell University.